BASKETBALL SKILLS FOR KIDS

Master Dribbling, Defense, Passing, Scoring, Teamwork, and More!

JACK RYDELL

Copyright 2025.

SPOTLIGHT MEDIA

ISBN: 978-1-951806-87-3

For questions, please reach out to:

Support@ActivityWizo.com

All Rights Reserved.

No part of this book may be reproduced or transmitted in any form or by any means, electronic or mechanical, including photocopying, recording, or by any other form without written permission from the publisher.

FREE BOOK

SCAN TO GET OUR NEXT BOOK FOR FREE

Table of Contents

INTRODUCTION 1

CHAPTER ONE: BASKETBALL 101 3

    A BRIEF HISTORY OF BASKETBALL 4

    THE VALUE OF BASKETBALL SKILLS 7

    WAYS YOU CAN PLAY BASKETBALL 9

    ENCOURAGEMENT AND MOTIVATION 11

    SAFETY TIPS 12

    TEAMWORK AND SPORTSMANSHIP 15

CHAPTER TWO: THE BASICS 19

    ALL ABOUT THE COURT 20

    CHOOSING THE RIGHT BASKETBALL AND SHOES 23

    BASKETBALL UNIFORMS 25

    PROTECTIVE GEAR 26

    MAINTAINING YOUR EQUIPMENT 27

    PACKING YOUR BASKETBALL BAG 29

CHAPTER THREE: WARM-UP AND CONDITIONING 33

    STRETCHING ROUTINES 34

    SIMPLE WARM-UP EXERCISES 36

    BASIC CONDITIONING EXERCISES 37

STAYING HYDRATED AND HEALTHY 40

COOLDOWN EXERCISES AFTER PLAYING 41

CHAPTER FOUR: DRIBBLING SKILLS 43

BASIC DRIBBLING TECHNIQUES 44

THE IMPORTANCE OF BALL CONTROL 46

DRILLS FOR IMPROVING DRIBBLING SKILLS 46

ADVANCED DRIBBLING MOVES 47

TIPS FOR CHANGING DIRECTION QUICKLY 49

PROTECTING THE BALL FROM DEFENDERS 50

CHAPTER FIVE: PASSING SKILLS 51

TYPES OF PASSES 52

PROPER PASSING TECHNIQUES 53

ACCURACY AND TIMING 54

DRILLS FOR IMPROVING PASSING SKILLS 55

EFFECTIVE COMMUNICATION WITH TEAMMATES 56

STRATEGIES FOR AVOIDING TURNOVERS 57

CHAPTER SIX: SHOOTING SKILLS 59

PROPER SHOOTING FORM AND TECHNIQUE 60

UNDERSTANDING SHOOTING MECHANICS 61

THE DIFFERENT TYPES OF SHOTS 61

DRILLS FOR PRACTICING DIFFERENT TYPES OF SHOTS . 63

FOOTWORK IN SHOOTING 65

SHOOTING UNDER PRESSURE 65

CHAPTER SEVEN: DEFENSIVE SKILLS 67

THE BASICS OF PLAYING DEFENSE 68

STAYING LOW AND BALANCED 69

TECHNIQUES FOR GUARDING OPPONENTS 69

BECOMING A GOOD DEFENSIVE PLAYER 71

BLOCKING SHOTS AND STEALING THE BALL 72

IMPROVING DEFENSIVE SKILLS 73

FOULS AND HOW TO AVOID THEM 74

CHAPTER EIGHT: REBOUNDING SKILLS 77

REBOUNDING IN BASKETBALL 78

POSITIONING AND TIMING FOR REBOUNDS 78

TECHNIQUES FOR OFFENSIVE AND DEFENSIVE REBOUNDING 79

DRILLS FOR IMPROVING REBOUNDING SKILLS 79

ANTICIPATING WHERE THE BALL WILL GO 80

STAYING MENTALLY FOCUSED 81

CHAPTER NINE: BOUNCING BACK FROM MISTAKES 83

LEARNING FROM MISTAKES 84

MAINTAINING FOCUS AFTER ERRORS 85

STAYING POSITIVE AND MOTIVATED 86

SUPPORT TEAMMATES AFTER A MISTAKE 87

DEVELOPING A GROWTH MINDSET 87

BUILDING RESILIENCE AND CONFIDENCE 88

CHAPTER TEN: GAME STRATEGIES AND TACTICS 91

UNDERSTANDING THE RULES OF BASKETBALL 92

BASIC OFFENSIVE AND DEFENSIVE STRATEGIES 94

READING THE GAME AND MAKING QUICK DECISIONS 95

COMMUNICATION AND TEAMWORK 97

DIFFERENT PLAYER POSITIONS AND ROLES 98

DEVELOPING A GAME PLAN WITH YOUR COACH 100

CHAPTER ELEVEN: MENTAL TOUGHNESS 103

MENTAL TOUGHNESS IN BASKETBALL 104

HANDLING PRESSURE AND STRESS 105

OVERCOMING MISTAKES AND SETBACKS 106

VISUALIZATION AND MENTAL REHEARSAL 107

DEALING WITH PERFORMANCE ANXIETY 107

USING RELAXATION TECHNIQUES 108

WHEN TO GET HELP 109

CHAPTER TWELVE: HEALTHY HABITS 111

NUTRITION YOUR BODY NEEDS 112

DON'T SKIP BREAKFAST! 114

FOODS TO EAT BEFORE A GAME 115

AWESOME SNACKS TO PACK 116

MANAGING YOUR TIME AND BALANCING LIFE 117

CHAPTER THIRTEEN: PLAYING WITH RESPECT AND GOOD SPORTSMANSHIP 119

RESPECTING OPPONENTS, COACHES, AND REFEREES . 120

HANDLING WINS AND LOSSES GRACEFULLY 121

BUILDING TEAM SPIRIT 122

DEALING WITH CONFLICTS 123

BEING A POSITIVE ROLE MODEL 123

LIFELONG BENEFITS OF PLAYING SPORTS WITH INTEGRITY 124

CHAPTER FOURTEEN: LEGENDS OF THE GAME 127

BASKETBALL SUPERSTARS.. 128

EPIC COMPETITIONS AND HISTORIC GAMES................... 129

RECORD-BREAKING MOMENTS 130

FAMOUS COACHES 131

LEGENDARY PLACES TO PLAY 132

IMPACT OF PLAYERS BEYOND THE COURT 133

CONCLUSION.. 135

INTRODUCTION

Basketball isn't just a game; it's a way to make friends, stay active, and become the leader you want to be. In this book, we'll start with the history of basketball, then move on to explain some of the skills you'll need and how to master them. This guide is appropriate for the absolute beginner or any player looking to improve their game.

You'll become an expert on the terminology, equipment, and skills you need to be a great basketball player. Being a good basketball player is more than skill; it means becoming a good teammate and building habits that enrich other parts of your life. This book will help you grow as a person and a player who sets an example both on and off the court.

So, lace up your sneakers and get ready to learn everything you need to know about succeeding on the court!

CHAPTER ONE: BASKETBALL 101

A BRIEF HISTORY OF BASKETBALL

Knowing how basketball developed can help you understand the game better. The more you know about the game, the better player you'll be!

Basketball had its start in 1891 at Springfield College's gymnasium, located in Springfield, Massachusetts. Before it was called Springfield College, the school went by the names School for Christian Workers, YMCA Training School, and International YMCA College.

This caused some confusion about the school and its relationship with the YMCA until documents found in 2010 cleared up the mystery: They showed that the building wasn't owned by the YMCA, but by the School for Christian Workers, which later became Springfield College, and the YMCA rented space in the large gym for activities.

Students often became restless during the long, cold months since they couldn't go outside and play sports. Massachusetts gets so much snow that many sports become impossible to enjoy. The physical education teacher, James Naismith, a 31-year-old, had a degree in theology but wanted to study physical education, which was rare at the time. As part of his continuing studies, Naismith was asked to create a new game that would be fun, easy to learn, and could be played indoors.

Naismith started looking at different sports and drawing inspiration from American and English rugby, soccer, lacrosse, and a game that Naismith had played as a child called "Duck on a Rock." His original thought was to use square boxes for the goals, but a janitor found peach baskets that were the perfect size. After he came up with 13 basic rules, the first trial game of basketball was played with those two baskets and a soccer ball.

The baskets were attached to the lower balcony at each end of the gym, where someone would stand during games to get the ball out and throw it back to the players. It took a few years before anyone thought to cut the bottoms out of the baskets!

Some of the original 13 rules were very different from what we know now, including how the ball was moved: dribbling wasn't allowed, so the ball had to be passed; there were nine players on the court instead of the five we watch today; and fouls looked different.

The Original 13 Rules of Basketball

1. The ball could be thrown in any direction as long as it stayed within bounds, using one or both hands.

2. The ball could be batted, similar to how a volleyball is hit, in any direction with one or both hands, but never with the fist.

3. Players couldn't run with the ball; once it was caught, the player had to stop moving, and then throw it from the spot where they caught it. However, it was okay if a player stumbled when they caught it.

4. The ball could only be held in or between the hands, not tucked under an arm.

5. Roughhousing was not allowed. Strike one caused a foul; the second strike disqualified a player until the next goal. If the violence was obviously intentional, the player was suspended for the entire game.

6. Fouls included hitting the ball with a fist and breaking rules 3, 4, or 5.

7. If either side made three fouls in a row, the other team received a point.

8. Goals were scored when the ball made it into the basket without bouncing out.

9. When the ball went out of bounds, the first player to get to it could throw it back in bounds. Whenever there was a disagreement, the umpire threw it back in. Each player had five seconds to throw the ball once they gained possession.

10. The umpire called all fouls and notified the referee when three fouls had been called in a row.

11. The referee decided when the ball was in bounds, which side had possession and kept time for the game. He also determined when a goal was made and kept track of the score.

12. Games lasted for two 15-minute halves, with a five-minute halftime.

13. At the end of the game, of course, the team with the most points won. In the event of a tie, the game continued until the next goal was scored.

The new game became a roaring success as soon as the rules were posted. Not only was it successful at Springfield College, but it also began to spread across YMCAs, and *College Magazine* published the rules.

By 1905, basketball was an officially recognized sport, spreading to other countries because of its popularity. Some rules changed over the years. For instance, in 1894, the soccer ball was traded for a specialty ball, and in 1906, metal hoops and backboards replaced the peach baskets. It wasn't until 1912 that cutting holes in the net became common practice.

While many rules have changed and others have been added in the years since basketball's creation, the sport remains very similar to what those bored young men played in that Springfield gym!

THE VALUE OF BASKETBALL SKILLS

If you love basketball and think you might want to play, the first step is to start developing your skills. Even with natural talent, you won't rise to be one of the best without hard work and dedication.

Whether you just enjoy playing with your friends, want to join a local team, or have plans to become a professional player, it all starts with basic skills. Dribbling, shooting, passing, and defending are things that every player needs to learn, and we'll discuss each of these — and more — in this book.

Basketball captivates millions of fans worldwide, and every fan would probably love to make a living at it or at least play regularly. However, it's only the players with the most honed and practiced skills who get the opportunity to make basketball their life.

Setting Goals

Whatever your motivation for playing basketball, whether it's to make the team, shoot three-pointers, or become famous, it all starts with setting goals. You need a clear vision of what you want to accomplish and which skills you need to get there.

However, it's important that you set specific goals, with a clear, measurable target. Goals like "I want to improve my shooting accuracy" or "I want to get better at defense" are all well and good, but without a way to measure your success, you'll never know if you've accomplished them!

Instead, fortify your desire to improve with clearly defined goals. For our previous examples, these might look something like "I aim to shoot with 80% accuracy" or "I will pass the ball five times in a game." When your targets are clearly defined, you can track your progress easily—and there's nothing better than the feeling of accomplishing a goal!

You also want to make sure your goals are achievable. If your goals are unrealistic, you'll only get discouraged. Saying, "I want to be the best basketball player in the world!" is admirable, but it doesn't make much sense in the short term.

Now, we're not saying you *can't* achieve big goals, but you'll have to give yourself years to accomplish them instead of expecting immediate success. In the meantime, set more practical goals that will help you improve over time. That way, you can celebrate your victories and stay motivated.

Another good practice is to keep each goal relevant to your current situation. While it's important to improve in all aspects of life, you can only focus on one thing at a time if you want to get better! It might be tempting to try to accomplish multiple goals all at once, but this often leads to burnout. Another common goal-setting mishap is to get caught up on future goals. Keeping goals relevant means focusing on what's most important right now. Start small and practice consistent improvement. The habits built this way will take you on to greater goals down the road.

The last step to achieving a good goal is to set a time limit for it. Don't set a goal that you want to be able to run a suicide in 25 seconds sometime in the future. Set your goal of wanting to run a 25-second suicide in the next month. That gives you the time frame in which you need to improve, and depending on how quickly you're improving, it lets you know how much practice you need to do.

WAYS YOU CAN PLAY BASKETBALL

There are many ways that you can get involved with basketball. Basketball doesn't always have to be played at a competitive level; it can be a wonderful casual sport as well.

One of the best ways to get started with basketball is to look for local youth programs. Community centers, churches, schools, and local organizations all offer basketball programs to get you on the court and start honing your skills.

One common organization you might consider is the YMCA, which has programs for young children. Your local recreation department is also another great place to check, and many churches are often involved in Upward or similar basketball programs.

Ask yourself several questions when looking to join a program in your community. Most require a small entrance fee but will waive it if you're unable to pay, so don't let that discourage you. Do your research about each program; most rely on volunteer coaches and have differing levels of skill and organization.

The more skills you gain, the more doors will open for you, allowing you to join more advanced teams. Many travel teams look for skilled players to see if they're a good fit for their team. These teams can be extremely competitive, though, so don't get discouraged or give up if you aren't selected for one.

More structured travel teams will help you develop your skills, which will allow you to try them out at school. Making the school team is a significant achievement because players are expected to have higher-level skills, and the coaches are more experienced.

Playing for your school involves aiming for titles, such as state and regional championships. School teams usually start in the 5th grade, which gives players a chance to start demonstrating their skills. In 6th grade, players move on to junior varsity (JV), and once high school comes around, it's time to join the varsity team and represent the entire school. Spots on school teams are highly sought after, so don't lose heart if you don't make the team — it just gives you more time to work on your skills!

If you want to improve, options are available to help increase your talent, like training camps — and this guide! Use your determination to drive your ability forward. Even once you age out of local groups and school teams, there are opportunities to pursue your passion for basketball.

Colleges are always looking for good players, and depending on your talents and strengths, some colleges offer scholarships to play for their school. Sports scholarships are a great way to pay for your education, giving you a chance to play the game you love *and* further your education.

Even if you don't find a college to play basketball for, you can still stay involved in the sport you love. Adults play pickup games all the time, and you can even join a league to stay involved. Not only can you continue to play, but volunteering to coach gives you a chance to pass on the knowledge and skills you worked so hard to learn.

ENCOURAGEMENT AND MOTIVATION

Basketball is an amazing sport with many positions and options for you to play. It doesn't matter whether you're tall or short, fast or still learning to be quick, basketball will welcome you as long as you enjoy playing.

Playing basketball doesn't just teach you to dribble, shoot, and pass; it will also teach you how to work as part of a team and give you the chance to make lifelong friends. Your team will celebrate wins and commiserate after a loss, whether on or off the court.

As you practice and put in the hard work that basketball requires, you'll find yourself falling in love with the sport. Every basketball player had to start somewhere, and even the best ballers in the world were beginners at some point.

Don't get discouraged by mistakes or how long it takes you to learn or improve on something. Every student of basketball moves at their own pace, and each time you practice, you'll get a bit more skilled, a bit stronger, and a bit faster. Just keep working hard.

When something discouraging happens, like missing a shot or letting someone score on you, don't let negative feelings rule out the amazing feeling you get from being out there on the court. Basketball should teach you to persevere—just keep pushing and moving forward!

Basketball is important not only on the court, but it also teaches lifelong health habits, mental conditioning, a sense of teamwork, and values. It's a wonderful stress outlet, a way to exercise, and provides a sense of accomplishment, whether you're playing competitively or just for fun. Knowing how amazing basketball is, go ahead and put on your sneakers, grab a basketball, and head to the court to start your journey!

SAFETY TIPS

While you're playing basketball, it's important to keep basic safety in mind. If you get injured, you'll be out of the season for however long it takes you to heal. During that time, you might miss important games or training.

Always Warm Up Properly

Taking time to stretch before you start playing gives your muscles a chance to prepare for physical activity. If you don't warm up, you have a greater chance of getting a sprain or straining a muscle. If that happens, you'll have to be benched, so be sure to take the time.

Wear the Right Gear

Good gear isn't determined by certain brands or styles; the clothing and shoes you wear on the court should be specifically made for basketball. Basketball shoes offer more support around the ankle than regular sneakers, guarding your ankles against sprains.

Drink Water!

It's easy to forget to stay hydrated when you're having fun or working hard, but water is essential for your body to function. You should always make sure to drink plenty of water before practice, during practice, and afterward.

Wear a Mouthguard

Some players choose to wear a mouthguard to protect their teeth. That is a personal choice that you should talk to your parents and coach about. It can be a good idea, especially if you have braces, to keep your mouth from getting cut up.

Learn Proper Techniques

You may have heard people say that you must learn to walk before you can run, and this applies to every sport, including basketball. Learning basic skills and proper form will cut down on injuries, both when you're starting out and throughout the rest of your basketball career.

Be Aware of Your Court

Play on safe surfaces, and make sure your court is free of trash or debris. It's easy to trip or sprain your ankle on a surface with lots of dips or holes. Uneven surfaces can also make it hard to control where you come down after a jump, so play on a court with as few obstacles as possible.

Avoid Overplaying

When you're in the heat of the game, it's easy to miss any warning signs your body might be giving you. If you start to feel nauseated, it's time to take a break and drink some water. Additionally, the more stressed out and tired you are, the more likely you are to get hurt.

Strength and Conditioning

Before jumping into a highly competitive situation, make sure you take the time to condition, so your body is prepared for the strain. Runners don't just wake up one day and decide to run a marathon; they spend time training to build up endurance and strengthen the muscles needed for running, and you should do the same.

Respect the rules

Among other things, rules are in place to keep unnecessary roughness off the court. When players get rowdy, people can get hurt.

Communicate with Your Teammates

To keep from hurting or embarrassing yourself, always be aware of where the other four members of your team are. There's nothing more embarrassing than running into a teammate!

Eat Right

Make sure you're giving your body the fuel it needs to excel on the court! Eating a balanced diet with the protein, vitamins, and minerals you need strengthens your body and keeps you healthy. Eating right also keeps your energy levels up when you need to be active.

Take Time to Cool Down

Just like before you play, make it a habit to stretch after practice and games to help your muscles recover. Stretching also helps prevent soreness the next day.

Wear Protective Padding

Depending on what position you play and your playing style, you might want to wear knee pads and long socks, as they provide protection if you hit the floor. Diving or leaping for the ball can be painful without them!

See Your Doctor

When you're playing any sport, you should have a physical check-up at least once a year. In fact, most organizations won't even let you play without a physical evaluation! Additionally, any time you feel lingering pain or soreness, you should make a special appointment to see your doctor.

Stay Mentally Focused

Keep your mind on the game, and don't get distracted by things going on in the stands or what might have happened during the day. You never know when a ball will come hurtling at your face, and while you're wondering what you're having for dinner later, you'll get smacked!

Listen to the Coach

It's your coach's job to tell you how to play safely and effectively. When you're on the court, it can be tempting to listen to fans yelling to do this or that, but the only instructions you should be focusing on during a game should come from your coach.

TEAMWORK AND SPORTSMANSHIP

One of the most rewarding aspects of basketball is the relationships you develop with your teammates. It's an amazing opportunity to interact socially and build friendships. Working toward a common goal builds camaraderie, providing a strong sense of support and belonging. You'll spend a lot of time with your team, so fellow teammates will become important in your life.

Basketball is a team sport, which means no one player can win on their own. No matter how talented you are, if it's you against five on the other team, you simply can't play to the best of your ability. When five players are guarding you, no amount of skill will get you past them.

You need your teammates, just like they need you, so learning to work as a team is vital. Luckily, there are many ways to show what a great teammate you are. Try passing the ball to open players, setting a screen to help someone get clear, or even just cheering for your team. A "Good job!" and a high five can do wonders for building confidence.

When everyone on the court plays together, it makes your entire team stronger. It's much more important to have five players working toward a common goal than one good player who will cost the game.

Sportsmanship is another part of being a good teammate. This involves being kind and respectful to everyone on the court. Good sportsmanship doesn't just mean respecting your coach and being nice to your teammates; it also means treating opponents, fans, and officials with respect.

During especially tough games, it can be hard to remember to demonstrate good sportsmanship, but that's when it's even *more* important. Tell the other team, "Good job" when they do well, and don't get mad at your teammates for making mistakes; it happens to everyone.

Everyone has seen that one player who gets mad, throws a fit, or starts yelling at someone. No one wants to play with people who act like that, and they're often transferred to other teams to avoid dealing with their behavior.

People probably won't remember an individual game years down the road, but they *will* remember how you acted during your basketball career. When you demonstrate good sportsmanship, your teammates will have more respect for you, fans will have a higher opinion of you, and refs will enjoy watching you play. At the end of the game, you'll feel better knowing you put your best foot forward.

While playing basketball, it's important to win, but having fun, playing hard, and supporting your fellow players will benefit you more in the long run. You'll have a reputation as an amazing player *and* person if you have the right attitude.

Teamwork and good sportsmanship aren't just important in basketball, though; they carry over into every part of your life. Whether you're working on a group project or accepting a promotion, being graceful and kind will earn you respect and admiration.

CHAPTER TWO: THE BASICS

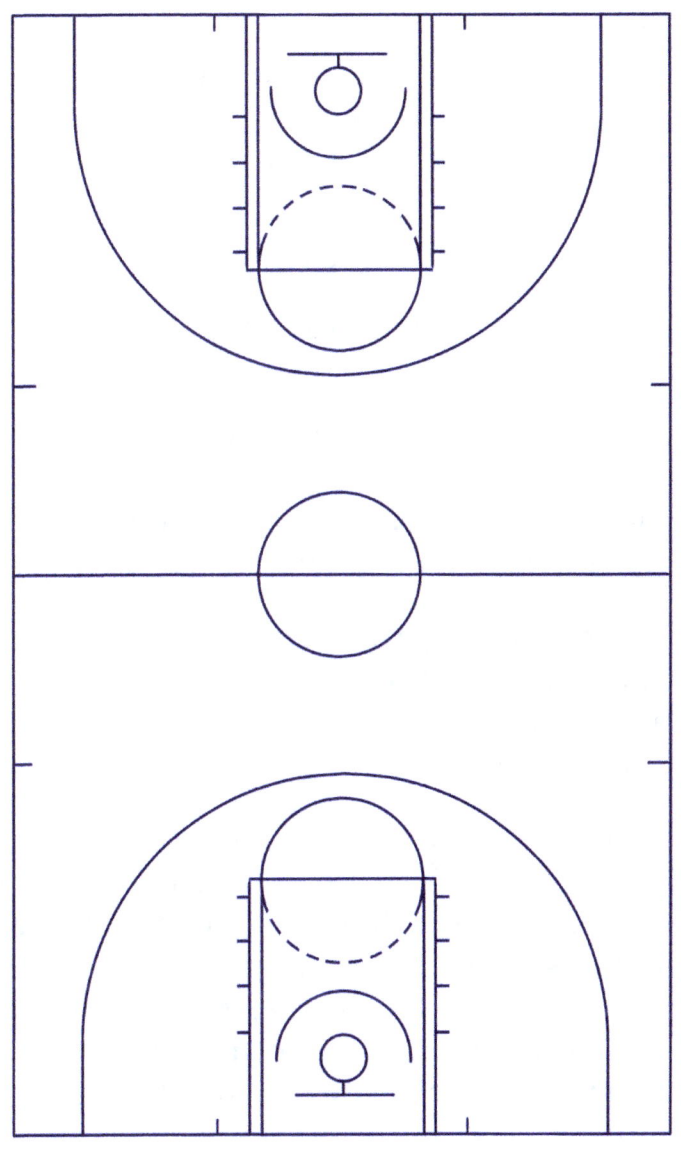

Having the right gear will help you succeed in basketball, but it doesn't have to be fancy. Wearing a certain name brand or style won't make you a better player—practice and hard work are what will give you long-lasting confidence that *things* can't give you.

While they don't have to be fancy, having the right tools for the job makes learning basketball much easier and can help you sprint down your basketball career path. As you improve and build your skills, you might need nicer equipment or more gear, but to start, all you need is a basketball and some tennis shoes!

ALL ABOUT THE COURT

Before you jump on the court, make sure you're familiar with its basic layout. Some of the information in this section might seem overwhelming for beginners. If you are confused, ask an adult to help you look up videos or take you to a court to get a visual.

Court measurements change depending on which level you play. The standard for a high school court is 85 feet x 50 feet; college is 90 feet x 50 feet; NBA is 94 feet by 50 feet; and international courts measure 28 meters x 15 meters.

The first important thing is the court itself. The lines on the floor can look crazy and confusing, but don't worry: They have a purpose, and learning what they mean is part of the game. There are a lot of terms to learn, and it might seem like a lot at first. However, it's important to know what the different areas on the court are called so that when your coach is telling you where to go, you aren't confused and can move quickly to the correct area.

The lines on the long side of the court form two sides of the rectangle, and they're called "sidelines." They mark the size of the court, which is usually 85 feet long. When the ball goes past those lines, it's "out," and the game stops.

The lines on the short sides of the court are called "endlines" or "baselines," depending on which team has the ball, and usually measure 50 feet. When the ball goes past these lines, it's also considered out of bounds.

Right in the middle is a line that cuts the rectangular court in half, known as the "midcourt" line. This line separates one team's side from the other's. When a team is on offense and they cross the midcourt line, they cannot go back across the line unless the other team touches the ball. Once a ball is live, it usually only takes about ten seconds for the offensive team to get the ball across the midcourt line.

The half circle that circles each goal is called the "three-point" line, and any goals shot from outside these lines are worth three points instead of two.

You'll also see a small circle directly in front of the goals with a line cutting it in half called the "free throw" line. When someone on the opposing team fouls a player while they're shooting, the team who was fouled is awarded a free throw (or "foul shot"), and that throw is taken from this line. Each free throw is worth one point. Appropriately, the circle around the line is called the free throw circle, and the shooter cannot leave that circle during a free throw.

The circle that is on the midcourt line is called the center circle. This is where the tip-off at the beginning of the game happens. The tip-off determines who gets the ball first, and one member of each team jumps for the ball and attempts to tip it to their team.

Lane lines mark the rectangle directly under the goal, which is usually a darker color than the rest of the court. They run from the endline to the free throw line, forming the "lane," sometimes known as the "paint" or "three-second" area. Offensive players are only allowed to stay in the lane for three seconds without getting the ball or stepping completely out and back into the circle.

There are a few other features on the court, too: Small rectangles on the lane lines mark where the players who aren't shooting should stand during free throws. In between the lines, players line up in defensive and offensive positions.

The 90-degree angle where the lane lines and free throw line meet is called the "elbow."

Two other important areas include the top of the three-point line and the top of the free throw circle. That area is called the top of the circle, or "key." Three-point shooters often shoot from this line and need to be guarded.

The far sides of the three-point line are called the "wings." Whichever side the ball is on is called the "ball-side," while the opposite wing is called the "weak-side."

The "corner" is near the goal, outside the three-point line but not out of bounds. It's a great area to trap an offensive player, leaving them nowhere to escape and forcing a turnover.

Along with a court, of course, you must have basketball hoops and backboards to play on. The hoops are how players score in basketball. Most backboards are rectangular or fan-shaped, and they're made from strong materials like tempered glass, acrylic, or polycarbonate. These materials allow the basketball to bounce off the backboard and—hopefully—into the hoop.

Each backboard has a square on it that allows the shooter to line up shots that will go in consistently. Once the ball heads to the hoop, it passes a metal ring with a rope net hanging from it. The various things that have been used over the years have formed some of basketball's slang, like hoops, baskets, and buckets.

Needless to say, other equipment—basketballs, shoes, uniforms, etc.—are essential parts of basketball, but the goal and court are what make this such a unique sport, so the more you know, the better prepared you'll be when you play.

CHOOSING THE RIGHT BASKETBALL AND SHOES

Several factors go into selecting basketball shoes, including support, cushioning, traction, size, and comfort.

Previously, it was believed that high-top shoes provided more support for your ankles, reducing the risk of sprains. However, shoes have changed a lot over the years, and research shows that this "support" doesn't actually have an impact on how often players sustain ankle injuries. High-top shoes can be heavier, but many larger basketball players prefer them.

Mid-top shoes aren't as high as high-tops and weigh a little less. They offer a great balance between support, weight, and flexibility. Low-top shoes are the lightest and offer the most flexibility and mobility, so they're good for players who move around a lot. Ultimately, it just comes down to which shoe you feel most comfortable in!

Make sure whatever shoes you choose have cushioning. You'll be jumping around a lot, so having something that will absorb the impact, keeping your joints from doing all the work, is easier on your body in the long run. You've got a lot of years ahead of you, and your body will appreciate you taking care of it! Look for shoes with advanced cushioning technology; they are extremely comfortable.

A good shoe will have a lot of traction on the court. If you're slipping and sliding, you won't be able to move quickly. Look for hexagonal patterns on the sole, and make sure the sole is a bit softer than what you normally wear. Don't wear your basketball shoes anywhere but in the gym, or you'll notice your shoes losing traction. Different shoes work better for outside basketball.

If your shoe doesn't fit, it won't provide you with the support or maneuverability that you need. If you have any special needs for your feet, like a wider shoe, make sure you look for that in your basketball shoe. Shoes that breathe well tend to be more comfortable and keep your feet from sweating as much—which everyone in the locker room will appreciate after a hard game!

Obviously, one of the most important things in the game is your basketball, and making sure that you have the correct kind is vital to your training.

Basketballs Come in Different Sizes:

Size 1: The micromini is 16 inches in circumference and is best for smaller children ages two to four. This is also the size of the collectible novelty balls.

Size 3: This mini basketball is for kids around four to six years old. It helps with skill development and coordination skills.

Size 4: Getting closer to basketballs used in games, size 4 is best for ages five to eight, and it's still pretty lightweight.

Size 5: This is the game ball size that you'll learn most of your skills with. It's ideal when transitioning to full-size basketball, helping with the development of skills like dribbling, shooting, and passing.

Size 6: Once you start middle school, you'll probably move up to a size 6. It's the size used in women's professional, college, and high school basketball, and it's the perfect weight for skilled maneuvers.

Size 7: This is the largest size of basketball and is only used by male players over the age of 15. Also called "official size," size 7 balls are used in the NBA.

BASKETBALL UNIFORMS

The first thing you need to consider for your uniform is your jersey. Schools and organizations have standard jerseys that reflect the team's colors. If you're playing community ball, having a practice jersey with a light side and a dark side will be sufficient.

Lightweight material that breathes well is best for jerseys because it keeps you from getting too hot. Besides being comfortable, jerseys will identify you as a player, displaying your number and team. Make sure your jersey is loose enough to allow you full range of motion. If your jersey prevents you from lifting your arms to shoot or makes it uncomfortable, go up a size.

Shorts are the next part of your uniform. Like your jersey, shorts should be loose-fitting and on the longer side. You want the same ease of movement so you can run and jump without being held up by your clothes! Elastic waistbands with drawstrings allow you to loosen and tighten shorts as needed, and a lot of shorts are made of the same breathable material as your jersey.

Once you've found out what your best shoe options are, it's time to think about what's going underneath: socks! Your socks should provide extra cushioning and reach up far enough that you don't get blisters. Extra padding also helps protect against rubbing when your feet get hot and sweaty.

Unlike your jersey and shorts, your socks should fit snugly, or they'll slide down in your shoes during practice or the game. Find socks that are tight enough not to slip, but not so tight that they cut off circulation.

There are a few other things you might want, depending on your needs, though they're optional. Compression gear is made to be worn under your uniform to provide extra support for various parts of your body. These are tights, sleeves, socks, shirts, or shorts that keep your muscles from getting sore, increase blood flow to prevent cramps, and even lessen the chance of strains and injuries.

If you find yourself constantly wiping sweat from your face or palms during a game, special headbands and wristbands can help. These are made from absorbent material to keep sweat from dripping into your eyes or making your hands too slick to catch the ball. As a bonus, they come in a variety of colors, giving you the chance to create a unique look on the court!

PROTECTIVE GEAR

In addition to a cool outfit, you might want some gear to provide extra comfort and support, including knee pads, protective eyewear, and knee or ankle braces. You don't have to wear protective gear, but it can keep you from getting hurt and missing out on games.

Knee pads are perfect for when you hit the ground diving for a jump ball or when you're trying to get possession before the other team.

Ankle and knee braces can help if you've injured yourself, and physical therapists and your doctors often recommend their use to prevent future injuries. You might also want to use these braces if you feel weakness in either area or are worried you might hurt yourself. You can use a brace as a temporary fix, but you should always see a doctor if you're concerned about your muscles or joints.

In basketball, you'll often find yourself scrambling for the ball; in these moments, it's all too easy to catch an elbow—or even a finger—in the eye. Because of this, many players use goggles to protect their eyes from injury. If you're worried about looking weird, just remember that famous basketball player Kareem Abdul-Jabbar wore goggles after sustaining several eye injuries! You may think goggles look silly, but they'll protect eyesight in the long run.

MAINTAINING YOUR EQUIPMENT

If you want your basketball gear to last, it's important to take care of it! A basketball might just seem like a round rubber ball that needs no special attention, but there are a few things you can do to keep it bouncing longer.

Store your ball in a cool, dry place out of direct sunlight. During summer and winter, you should bring it inside—extreme temperatures will cause the rubber to lose its bounce over time. If your basketball starts warping or cracking, it's time to retire it and look for a new one.

Wipe down your basketball after every practice to remove dirt, germs, and sweat. Don't try to give your ball a bath, though! Just a wet rag with some mild soap will do the job.

Over time, air will escape from even the tightest seal, so it's important to refill your ball from time to time. When you push on your ball, it should hardly sink in at all, so make sure there's a hand air pump with a ball needle available to inflate it.

Keep in mind that an overinflated ball will bounce too much, and an underinflated ball won't bounce enough. Check your ball by dropping it from shoulder height — it should bounce back to about hip height. If it's lower, add air, and if it's higher, let some air out.

Sports come with some funky smells, and shoes get the worst of it. Taking care of your shoes after practice and games can help keep that stink down *and* make your shoes last longer. After a sweaty practice or game, dry your shoes completely by taking the insole out and putting the shoes somewhere they can air out. Don't just leave your gym bag at the bottom of your closet with no airflow!

If you find that your shoes aren't drying completely, try putting newspaper or paper towels in there to absorb moisture. Don't use hair dryers, radiators, or other heat sources to speed up the process, though — just as with your basketball, too much heat can damage your shoes.

If your basketball shoes get dirty, use a damp cloth to wipe them off. It's best to do this regularly so the grime doesn't build up. You should also wash your insoles occasionally to prevent bacteria buildup, which is a big source of odor. Store your shoes somewhere dry and cool, not outside or in a bathroom with lots of humidity, because they'll never get dry!

Wash your uniform in cold water to keep the colors bright. You can use laundry detergent but don't add bleach. When it's washed, hang it up to dry instead of putting it in the dryer so the vinyl doesn't get damaged. Hang it on a hanger and put it in your closet after it's dry.

Compression gear, headbands, and wristbands also need to be washed after every use. Wash them the same way as your uniform, with cold water, and hang them to air-dry.

PACKING YOUR BASKETBALL BAG

When you're playing at home or in your local court, having everything on hand isn't a huge priority because home is close by. However, when you head out of town for games or tournaments, you need to make sure you have everything with you.

You'll need your uniform, shoes, socks, and anything you wear under your uniform. Make sure you have a water bottle, a face towel for wiping away sweat, deodorant to put on before and after the game, hand wipes to disinfect your hands as needed, and a small first aid kit. You might also want to pack some healthy snacks for after the game.

In your first aid kit, make sure you have hydroperoxide—if you get scratched and bleed, the blood on your uniform will keep you from playing. The good news is that hydroperoxide is great for getting blood out of clothes.

Before the game, you'll probably need warm-up or cover-up clothes. After the game, you'll want to change and put on different shoes, so you aren't walking anywhere but on the court with your basketball shoes.

Pack your basketball, any compression gear, braces, headbands, wristbands, knee pads, or any other protective gear you wear. A phone and charger to get in touch with your parents after the game and some money for concession stands are also good things to have.

In the excitement of getting ready and then leaving after the game, some of your gear might accidentally end up stuck in someone else's bag. If you label everything in your gym bag with your name, though, they'll know it's yours, and it will help you get your gear back.

Here's a checklist you can use to double-check your bag:

- Jersey
- Shorts
- Basketball shoes
- Socks
- Under-uniform items
- Water bottle
- Healthy snacks
- Face towel
- Deodorant
- Hand wipes
- Hand sanitizer
- First aid kit
- Hydroperoxide
- Mouthguard
- Warm-up clothes
- Clothes for after the game
- Extra shoes to wear off-court

- Basketball
- Hand-held pump and needle
- Compression gear
- Braces
- Headbands
- Wristbands
- Goggles
- Phone
- Charger
- Extra money
- Extra bag for sweaty clothes and shoes

CHAPTER THREE: WARM-UP AND CONDITIONING

Wearing the right gear and honing your skills is important for staying in shape and playing your best game, but what you do right before and right after a game is just as important!

Taking time to warm-up before playing basketball prepares your body for physical activity. One benefit is increased blood flow to your muscles, which ensures you're getting the oxygen and nutrients you need to prevent cramps. Warming up also raises the temperature of your muscles—thus the term "warm-up"—increasing flexibility, which means you're less likely to get a strain or tear.

Players that warm-up tend to play better and get into the rhythm of the game faster. After a warm-up, players tend to have better reaction times and better coordination. Your strength and power are also affected by whether your muscles are warm or not.

Physical ability isn't the only factor that comes into play when playing basketball. It's important to be mentally prepared as well because focus and concentration make a better player. You need to be mentally sharp and ready to make quick decisions while being aware of where your teammates are.

Having a routine to start every game or practice also makes your team work together more smoothly. There can even be a certain amount of intimidation associated with your warm-up. When another team sees your team working together perfectly with a well-done warm-up drill, they start to get nervous about playing against you.

STRETCHING ROUTINES

Before you do anything else, you need to stretch. Most basketball injuries occur in the ankles, feet, knees, thighs, and hips, so it's important to focus on stretching in those areas to lessen the chances of injury.

There are two types of stretching: static and dynamic. Static stretching involves holding a stretch for an extended period of time. This type of stretching isn't great for a pregame warmup, but it's perfect for after the game.

Pregame, you want to focus on dynamic stretching, which is about using your muscles fully but not holding a stretch for too long.

Here are some good ways to stretch dynamically before the game. Start on the end line, go all the way to midcourt, and do each of these exercises two or three times:

> **High Knee Jogging:** Jog up and down the court, raising your knees as high as possible, to get your heart pumping faster.
>
> **Butt Kicks:** Jog back and forth, kicking your heels up and hitting your buttocks. This movement warms up the hamstrings.
>
> **Leg Swings:** With one hand against a wall for balance, swing one leg forward and then back as far as you comfortably can, about 10-15 times for each leg. Next, put your back against the wall and do the same thing, except side to side in front of you.
>
> **Walking Lunges:** Step forward and bend your knees at a 90-degree angle. Then do the same with the other leg and repeat about 10 times.
>
> **Arm Circles:** Put both arms straight out to your sides and make small circles. Do 10 clockwise and 10 counterclockwise, moving both arms at the same time.

Knee Hugs: Walk forward, and with each step you take, pull one leg up to your chest and hug with both arms. Repeat 10 times for each leg.

Defensive Slides: Separate your legs and squat down until your knees are at a 90-degree angle, like you're guarding someone, then shuffle to midcourt and back two times.

SIMPLE WARM-UP EXERCISES

Basketball drills, cardiovascular activity, and skill practice are important parts of a good warmup. Below, we've listed several pregame exercises that aren't too strenuous, but they're good to use in practice to push yourself more. You can do any of these alone, but they're easier with multiple people.

Layup Lines: Start at midcourt and dribble down to the lane. Next, pick up the ball and take a step to lay the ball onto the backboard with the same side hand as the hand you're shooting with. Do this twice before a game and as many times as you can during practice.

Dribbling: A good way to build skills or get ready for a game is "suicide dribbling." Start at the end line with a ball, dribble with your dominant hand to the free throw line, turn around and come back, go to the end line, turn and go to the midcourt, and turn to return to the end line. Before a game, you can just do half the court, but during practice, complete the whole court multiple times as fast as you can go. Time yourself and push yourself to get faster.

Shooting: Start at the bottom right corner of the lane, move to the top corner, take a free throw shot, move to the next corner, and finally, to the bottom corner. Before a game, do this once, but during practice, do it as many times as you can.

Each coach will have their own pregame routine, so follow your coach's instructions. However, these are great exercises to do on your own time, and you'll probably see them pregame.

BASIC CONDITIONING EXERCISES

There are different practice drills for different skills you'll need as a basketball player. You'll need to be able to run, be agile, and possess strength and endurance. Here are some different drills you can use to improve those skills and your overall athletic ability. Remember, not everyone is a natural athlete; it's a skill you must develop like any other.

Running Drills

To have a successful career in basketball, you must be able to run up and down the court. The faster you get down the court, the more time you have to set up, get open, or prepare for defense. No matter how amazing you are, if you're the last player down the court every time, you'll be too late to help your team.

Suicides: Start on the end line and run to the following lines in this order: free throw, back to baseline, midcourt, back to the end line, opposite free throw, back to baseline, to the opposite end line, then back to the starting end line.

Full-Court Sprints: Instead of stopping at every line, start at one end line, sprint to the opposite side, and continue for a set number of times or amount of time.

Lane Slide: Start on one sideline and use a defensive slide to travel to the other and back again. Continue for however many, however long, or until you can't do anymore!

Agility Drills

Agility drills are designed to speed up your footwork, allowing you to move more nimbly across the court. The faster you can move and the more quickly you maneuver, the easier it is for you to dodge opponents.

Shuttle Runs: Start at the end line and sprint to the midcourt, touch the line, and without turning around, run backward, returning to the end line.

Cone Drills: Set up a few cones in any spacing or order and run between each one. You can do this while dribbling or without a ball, moving as quickly as you can.

Ladders: You need an exercise ladder for this drill, which you'll lay on the floor. The goal is to get one foot in each space as quickly as possible. Then, try to hop two feet into each space. You can even graduate to going sideways as quickly as possible.

Strength and Endurance Workouts:

While you could always lift weights or work out at the gym, you'll need to speak to a gym teacher, your parents or guardians, and your doctor before starting a weightlifting routine. You're still growing and lifting weights can actually be harmful if you do it incorrectly. These are some on-court exercises that build up your muscles without weights:

Jump Rope: Jump in two-minute intervals several times to help you build up leg strength and endurance.

Planks: Start on the floor, putting all your weight on your palms and the balls of your feet with your body perfectly straight, like a wood plank, and hold for a set amount of time.

Push-ups: Start in a plank position with your arms straight, lower yourself until your elbows are bent 90 degrees, and then push back up, never letting any part of your body touch the ground except your hands and the balls of your feet.

Squats: Focusing on leg strength, stand straight and then squat down until your knees are bent at a 90-degree angle, then slowly push back up. Moving slowly is the key to this exercise, as it forces your muscles to work harder.

Tuck Jumps: To improve your jumping and rebounding abilities, you need to get used to jumping as high as possible. For this exercise, jump as high as you can, tucking your knees to your chest while in the air, then get them back down to land.

Lateral Bounds: Focus on jumping up as hard as you can on one leg and coming down on the other, then jump as high as you can on that leg. Repeat the exercise, focusing on getting as high as possible.

Bicycle Crunches: Lay back and bend your knees, with the back of your feet almost touching your buttocks. Sit up and touch your elbow to the opposite knee, switching between them while never laying back down. When you do this, your legs will naturally make cycling motions.

STAYING HYDRATED AND HEALTHY

If you get dehydrated, your performance on the court will suffer. Proper hydration allows you to maintain high energy for longer periods and mentally focus under pressure, and it prevents cramps and overheating. Drinking water is great, but sometimes adding sports drinks can help—though many have unnecessarily high sugar levels, so you have to be careful.

Water makes up about 60 percent of your body, and if you sweat out too much without replacing it, you'll become dehydrated. Dehydration causes headaches, fatigue, and muscle cramps that can ruin your game.

You should drink primarily water during practice and games. Staying hydrated means you maintain a healthy body temperature and keep nutrients moving throughout your body. Don't just drink water at basketball, though! Your body *always* needs water, so make it a habit to carry some with you.

Sports drinks can be helpful because they contain electrolytes like sodium and potassium, both of which are excreted when we sweat. You need those nutrients to prevent cramping. However, as we mentioned, many so-called "sports drinks" contain unnecessary ingredients—particularly sugar—so do your research! Try drinking sports drinks during the middle of games and practice and stick to water the rest of the time.

Times it is most important to drink water:

- Two to three hours before a game, make sure to drink at least 16 ounces of water.
- During games, drink at least ten ounces of water every 20 minutes.
- At halftime, try drinking sports drinks along with water.
- If you get a break during an intense part of the game—like when your coach calls a timeout, or you sub—try drinking some more sports drinks.
- After the game, drink a sports drink, then drink as much water as possible.

Using both sports drinks and water together is the best way to stay hydrated. However, remember that your body is made up of water, not sports drinks, so drink more water!

COOLDOWN EXERCISES AFTER PLAYING

Slowly cooling down after a hard practice or game prevents muscle soreness and prepares for your next basketball adventure!

Jogging or walking around after heavy physical activity is a good way to let your muscles cool down. Jog around for about five minutes, then slow to a walk for a few minutes more. Don't sit still immediately after working out—your muscles will stiffen up.

Here are some nice, light stretches for your cooldown routine:

Hamstring Stretch: Sit on the ground with one leg out straight and the other bent. Reach for your toes, keeping your leg straight, and hold for 30 seconds, then switch legs.

Quadriceps Stretch: Stand on one leg and use one hand to pull the opposite foot to your buttocks. Hold for 30 seconds and repeat on the other leg.

Calf Stretch: Put your hands on a wall and stretch one foot back, pushing your heel toward the ground. Hold for 20-30 seconds, then switch.

Shoulder Stretch: Pull one arm across your chest and fold the other over it, pulling tight. Hold for 20-30 seconds, then switch arms.

Triceps Stretch: With one arm, reach over your back, putting your hand between your shoulder blades and putting your other hand on your elbow to pull further. Hold for 20-30 seconds.

A hot soak with Epsom salt and a light massage can help sore muscles after an intense workout.

CHAPTER FOUR: DRIBBLING SKILLS

Dribbling is a vital skill that players need to move the ball around the court, get around defenders, and create scoring opportunities.

BASIC DRIBBLING TECHNIQUES

So, what exactly *is* dribbling, anyway? To put it simply, dribbling is bouncing the ball against the court. You must dribble to move the ball down the court, so that means you must use those skills any time you want to move to a better shooting position, get out of a crowded area, or drive to the basket.

The fundamentals of dribbling are essential for every basketball player since it's the only way you can move the ball down the court. As you know, the more you control the ball, the more you control the game. The best ball handlers set the pace of the game along with the direction the team will be going.

Some things to keep in mind when you're dribbling include making sure you don't look down—it's important to stay aware of the court. Keep your knees bent and your back straight, with your arm out as a shield. This is called the "triple threat" position and will be your go-to or "home" position when you start dribbling.

Don't ever let the ball touch your palm while you're dribbling—use your fingers! If you let the ball touch your palm when it's coming up, you lose maneuverability. If you flip your hand under the ball while dribbling, it's considered a "carry," and you'll lose possession of the ball.

Always use force while dribbling; you want the ball to return to your hand as quickly as possible, so it needs enough force behind it to bounce back up.

Here are several techniques you need to master:

Stationary Dribbling: One way to practice is to stand in one place, dribbling over and over with each hand. You'll probably be naturally more coordinated with one hand, but you need to be able to dribble with both! Start with your knees slightly bent, about shoulder-width apart. Always keep your head up; if you're having to watch the ball, you need to keep working at it.

Control Dribble: This is all about keeping the ball close, focusing on using your fingertips and not your palm to keep control of the ball. Having the ball close allows you to slip through defenders much easier. Keep the ball below waist level to make it harder for someone to reach in and take it from you. Always keep your non-dribbling arm up to shield the ball and stay in the triple threat position. This speed of dribbling is suited for slow-to-medium speed.

Speed Dribble: When getting down the court is your goal, moving quickly while pushing the ball out in front of you can help you cover the court more quickly. When moving this fast, the ball will come up higher, but if it goes to chest level, you don't have enough control. This technique is used for a fast break when you're trying to beat everyone else down the court and score before the defense can set up.

Pound Dribbling: Squat down, dribbling as hard and as fast as you can, and keep the ball knee level or lower. Remember to practice with both hands!

THE IMPORTANCE OF BALL CONTROL

Dribbling cannot be stressed enough as a basketball skill. It's one of the most important skills for a player to have.

Having a good ball handler reduces turnovers, taking away the other team's chances to score. Guards, especially your point guard, must be expert dribblers. Their job is to get the ball across the midcourt and start a play, maintaining the ball until everyone gets in position and someone is open to receive a pass.

When dribbling the ball, the responsibility for creating space and drawing the defenders in a direction to open up other players will fall to you. Once you pick up the basketball, you can't put it back down or start dribbling again. If you do, it's considered "double dribbling" and will result in a turnover for the other team.

No matter how good you are, if you can't handle the ball, you'll spend a lot of time on the bench. Take the time to improve your dribbling sooner rather than later because it will improve your value on the court.

DRILLS FOR IMPROVING DRIBBLING SKILLS

There are drills you can practice to improve your dribbling. Even if you're already skilled, these drills can take your skill to the next level and make you even more dangerous on the court.

The Figure-Eight Drill: You don't need anything but a basketball for this drill. The goal is to dribble through your legs. Start at one ankle and dribble through your legs, then switch to the other hand and continue around the other leg. It's important to keep your knees bent while doing your figure eight.

Back and Forth Drill: Start dribbling with your right hand and have your left up as a shield. Dribble forward five steps, like you have a defender in front of you, then backward five steps. Repeat with the other hand and continue to switch back and forth. Remember to keep your head up!

Two-Ball Dribbling: You need two balls to practice this move. Start by standing still and dribbling with both hands at the same time. Once you feel comfortable, start walking and gradually increase your speed. Eventually, you'll be able to sprint down the court while dribbling both balls!

Catch Behind the Back: While not technically dribbling, this exercise helps sharpen your reflexes. Start with the ball in both hands, directly behind your back, and drop the ball. Quickly reach behind your lower back and catch the ball mid-fall. Keep working at it until you can catch the ball consistently.

Partner Dribble: Inside a set area, like the lane, two people dribble while trying to steal the other's ball. This drill helps you focus on keeping your attention on what is going on around you instead of staring down at the ball.

ADVANCED DRIBBLING MOVES

Once you've mastered basic dribbling techniques, you'll want to start learning the advanced moves that will allow you to get out of tight spots and evade defenders. If you have any interest in being a point guard, you'll be expected to have a high level of skill with the ball.

Some moves you can use are the crossover, behind the back, spin move, in-and-out dribble, double cross, offensive box out, and hesitation dribble. You might notice that you're already practicing some of these moves in your drills!

> **Crossover:** One of the most common tricks you'll use when dribbling is crossing the ball from one hand to another to keep it where you want it. This helps when you're trying to get by a defender or change directions.
>
> **Behind the back:** Just like the crossover, behind the back is designed to get the ball away from a defender, but instead of crossing in front, you cross in the back to keep the ball safe.
>
> **Spin Move:** This move requires great ball control, but it allows you to turn 360 degrees to scope out the court while maintaining control of the ball. It also gives you a chance to change direction.
>
> **In-and-Out Dribble/Fake Move:** With this move, you're trying to trick your defender by acting like you're going for a crossover, but instead, sending the ball back to the original hand.
>
> **Double Cross:** To attempt a breakaway from your defender in the direction you're already going, you can crossover the ball and commit to it—but at the last second, instead of moving that direction, cross the basketball back over and continue in your original direction.

Offensive Box Out: While dribbling the ball, get your back to the defender, and you can use your rear to hold them off you, forcing them to guard from behind.

Hesitation Dribble: When you first receive the ball, pretending to pass or shoot the ball makes the defender move in that direction, which leaves you open to make a break in the opposite direction. Just remember, you can't pick up the ball from dribbling and then start dribbling again!

TIPS FOR CHANGING DIRECTION QUICKLY

It's important to be able to change direction without losing control of the ball when you're cornered by defenders or need to get to an open spot for shooting and passing.

When you're ready to change directions, make sure your body center is low, knees bent, with your weight on the balls of your feet, not the heels. Staying on the balls of your feet allows you to pivot swiftly and not be "flat-footed," which makes you slower.

Once you've decided to change directions, don't project or make your intentions obvious. If you keep looking in that direction, a good defender will follow your eyes and know what's coming. Be explosive when you pivot and catch your defender off guard.

Make sure you plant your outside foot, keeping your knees bent, then push off your planted foot and keep the ball as close to you as possible. Use a crossover to put the ball on the side away from the defender. This is where the practice of crossing between your legs, behind your back, and in front of you comes into play.

PROTECTING THE BALL FROM DEFENDERS

The most basic way to protect the ball from the other team is to use the triple threat position, so it should be the first thing you perfect as a basketball player. To get into the triple threat position, lower your center of gravity, keep your back straight and knees bent, and place your weight on the balls of your feet.

Start the ball with both hands tucked against your hips and keep your body between the ball and your defender. Keep your head up and your feet spread out, so you won't trip. When you're ready to dribble, your non-dribbling hand should serve as a bar to keep anyone from grabbing the ball. This is the position that allows you the most flexibility.

Keep your speed changing and don't be predictable; that way, defenders will have a hard time guarding you, and you'll have more opportunity for passes and shots.

CHAPTER FIVE: PASSING SKILLS

Moving the basketball around the court requires a specialized skill called passing. Players can't run with the ball without dribbling, and the ball can't be dribbled once it's picked up, so passing is how you get the ball where it needs to go.

TYPES OF PASSES

There are several types of passes, including the chest pass, bounce pass, overhead pass, and one-handed pass.

Chest pass: This pass is for passing straight, and it's the best way to start learning. While this pass is great for moving the ball around the court, it won't get you past defenders because the ball stays at arm level, making it easy to swat out of the air.

To do a chest pass, start in a triple threat position and hold the ball at your hip. Always call out the name of the person you're passing to. It's a good habit to establish because it lets your teammate know the ball is coming their way. Put power behind the throw so it'll reach your teammate quickly, reducing the chance that an opponent will knock it down or get to it before your teammate.

Bounce Pass: This is like a chest pass, but instead of going straight across, the ball bounces once before reaching its destination. This pass is good for getting past defenders because it drops the ball out of reach, making it tougher to stop. A bounce pass works well when a defender is right on top of you. As with the chest pass, start in the triple threat position and make sure to alert your teammate that the ball is coming their way.

Overhead Pass: If you need to cover long distances, this is the way to go! However, it's not a great pass to use if there's anyone between you and your teammate because, as you know basketball players can jump, so they can grab the ball out of the air.

One-Handed Pass: This pass is similar to a chest pass but with one hand. You'll need to master the chest pass before you move on to this pass, though, because the release is quicker; It works well for fast-paced situations.

PROPER PASSING TECHNIQUES

Chest Pass: Pull the ball up to your chest with both hands. Point your fingers toward the receiver, and step in the direction you're passing with your elbows close to your body. Then, extend your arms and let go of the ball with a snap of your wrist. Follow through with another step, palms facing away from each other, pointing at the floor with your thumbs.

Bounce Pass: Start just like a chest pass, but don't aim for your teammate's chest. Instead, aim for the floor. Throw it two-thirds of the way—not halfway, but just past that point. Otherwise, your form should be exactly like the chest pass.

Overhead Pass: Straighten from the triple threat position and hold the ball up with both hands over your head. Call your teammate and step forward, bringing your arms back, then release the ball with a snap of the wrist. Make sure your hands wind up with your palms facing outward, just like the previous passes.

One-Handed Pass: Start with the ball at your hip in a triple threat position. Put your dominant hand behind the ball for power, with the other on the side for control. Step and pass the ball, aiming for your teammate's chest. Just like the other passes, make sure you wind up with an extended thumb pointing to the floor.

ACCURACY AND TIMING

On the court, sometimes the timing and accuracy of your throw will make or break a play. Accuracy is important for many reasons. You can only maintain possession if you're accurate with your passes, as badly aimed passes go to the other team — giving them a chance to score.

Accuracy also helps with offensive plays because they rely on the ball getting to the intended player, and sometimes you'll even need to be accurate enough to put the ball where your teammates *will* be, instead of where they *are*. When you lead with the ball, you're thinking about getting ahead of a teammate who's moving fast.

Well-placed passes can open up scoring opportunities that your team might not have otherwise — especially when you're playing against a team with a great defense and getting off the shot is hard.

Timing is just as important as accuracy; if you pass at the wrong time, no matter how accurate the pass is, the ball still won't make it to your teammate! Timing is also an important factor in exploiting defensive gaps, allowing you to take advantage of opportunities you wouldn't otherwise be able to exploit.

This comes into play for making fast breaks, which are an important part of a good offense. Fast breaks involve getting down the court quickly to score before the opposing team can set up a proper defense. Passing during fast breaks requires coordination with your teammates, which means perfect timing is essential.

DRILLS FOR IMPROVING PASSING SKILLS

These passing drills are designed for your whole team. Practice each of these drills until you're comfortable with them; then, you can move on to more advanced drills.

Circle Drill: Have six to eight players stand in a circle, with one teammate in the middle. That person starts with the ball and then passes it to a teammate who immediately passes it back. This continues in random selection for 15 or so passes before another teammate gets in the middle.

Full Court Passing: Split up into two teams of five and spread everyone out on the court. The goal is for the team to pass with their five players, never dribbling until they score. At the same time, the other team will be trying to intercept passes, and if they do, *that* team passes until they score. The first team to score five points (or the team with the most points after a set amount of time) wins.

Three-Point Line Swing: Have five players line up around the three-point half circle. Start with no defenders so you and your teammates can get a feel for what you're doing; once you do, add defenders to put pressure on the offense. Start at the top with the point guard, and practice passing the ball around the half circle to get it from one side to another.

Three-Man Maneuver: Line three teammates up on the end line and have the one in the middle start with the ball. They'll pass to one of the outside players, then run behind the player while they sink to the middle. That player then passes to the other side and runs behind *that* player after they pass. Continue weaving up the court until you reach the other end line.

Moving Target: Pair up and stand across from your partner at the end line, about 15 feet apart. Travel down the court, passing back and forth, and work on leading your partner, throwing where they *will* be instead of where they *are*, so neither of you has to slow down for the ball.

EFFECTIVE COMMUNICATION WITH TEAMMATES

Communicating with your team will become more important as the complexity of your plays increase. Verbal cues are the easiest way to get your teammates' attention on the court. Yelling, "I'm open!" or "Here!" will let your teammates know you're open, so they can pass you the ball. When you want to pass the ball, yelling your teammate's name gives them a heads-up that the ball is coming their way, even if you aren't looking at them.

However, if you're worried about the other team picking up on your verbal cues (especially if they know your teammates' names), nonverbal options work best. Eye contact is one easy way to let someone know the ball is passing. The best thing to do, though, is to prepare ahead of time, coming up with hand signals to communicate with your team. This is especially useful for point guards when they want to call a play as they bring the ball down the court.

Keep in mind that, for communication to be effective, your team must *want* to hear what you're saying. Offering positive feedback, like "Good job!" or "Nice pass!" encourages your teammates to be receptive. If all you ever have is negative feedback, like "Why did you do that?" or "Come on!" they won't want to listen to you on the court.

When using verbal communication, make sure you speak clearly, and loud enough to be heard! If your teammates can't hear you, it won't do any good. Gyms can be very loud during games, with fans yelling and sounds echoing.

Come together as a team before games to make sure you're all on the same page, so everyone understands how to communicate as a team.

STRATEGIES FOR AVOIDING TURNOVERS

One of the biggest challenges you'll face when passing is avoiding turnovers, which can easily give the other team points that lose the game. To avoid losing possession, make smart passes! If the pass is tricky, keep moving the ball until you find another opening. Cross-court is almost always a bad idea because the chance of interception is so high.

Fake passes to throw off your defender can give you a second to get a real pass off if you're covered up and can't get the ball out. Pretending to throw the ball to your right, then quickly passing to your left is a great example of a fake pass. Don't always use the same fake, though, or it will lose its effectiveness over time.

Staying spaced out is also important; if everyone is bunched together on one side of the court, there's no way for someone to get open for the pass. Congestion hinders your team and helps the defense.

Keep your passes sharp and fast. After all, it's hard to stop a fast-moving ball! If your teammate is on the move, lead them with the ball so the ball ends up where they're going, not where they were.

Another strategy is pivoting; once you stop dribbling and pick up your ball, you can't move again, but you can plant one foot and use it as a pivot to move your other foot in a circle while you look for open teammates.

CHAPTER SIX: SHOOTING SKILLS

Obviously, the only way to win a game is to score more points than your opponents. While a good defense is important, you also have to be able to score! In this chapter, we're going to give you a rundown of shooting techniques, along with some drills you can practice to improve your shooting game.

PROPER SHOOTING FORM AND TECHNIQUE

Step one to a good shot is to set it up correctly. Stand with your feet shoulder-width apart for balance, and make sure both feet are pointing straight ahead. Put whatever hand you write with (your "dominant" hand) forward a little bit, and plan to shoot with that hand. Bend your knees slightly and put your weight on the balls of your feet instead of your heels.

Hold the ball firmly, with your fingers spread out wide. Your dominant hand goes under and behind the ball to support it, forming an *L* shape. Don't palm the ball but use your finger pads to hold it. Put your other hand on the side, not holding the ball but providing balance.

Keep your shooting elbow under the ball, lined up with your body, with your shoulders directly over your knees. Keep your eyes locked on the spot you want your ball to go. If you aren't looking when you shoot, chances are, the ball won't go in.

When you're ready to shoot, lift the ball up smoothly and extend your arm toward the basket. As you release the ball, snap your wrist, almost like you're waving goodbye to the ball. Hold that stance until the ball is gone, and don't move your guide hand while shooting. It isn't providing power; use that hand for balance and guiding the ball.

Use your legs and core muscles to provide extra power to the ball if you need it. As you might suspect, it takes more muscle to shoot from the three-point line than from under the goal, so know your strengths and where you shoot best.

Practice makes perfect, so mastering shooting will take a while. If you want to be an amazing shooter, plan to take 250 or more shots at every practice.

UNDERSTANDING SHOOTING MECHANICS

When you shoot the ball, aim to do one of these two things:

Arc: When you're shooting from a distance or an angle where you can't use the backboard, it's important to have a lot of arc on your ball. Waving goodbye to the ball gives it some backspin, which makes it more likely to follow your intended path. Additionally, if it hits the rim, backspin can help it get into the ring.

Use the backboard: When you're closer to the basket, you can use the backboard instead of aiming straight for the ring. The square on the backboard allows you to aim more precisely, and hitting the right spot while your ball is spinning is called "banking" a shot. When you're shooting from the block under the goal on the right side, you should aim for the top right corner of that square, and the spin should send your ball directly into the ring.

THE DIFFERENT TYPES OF SHOTS

Layup: A layup is when you try to "lay" the ball onto the backboard. To perform this one-handed maneuver, shoot with the hand on whichever side of the goal you're on. It doesn't matter if you're right-handed when shooting a left-handed layup; you must use your left hand.

Start outside the lane and dribble to the goal with your outside hand. Take two steps, then release the ball onto the backboard.

Jump Shot: One of the more common basketball shots, the jump shot involves stopping and jumping while shooting. This shot works from anywhere on the court, and the sudden stop helps gain space from defenders.

Three-Point Shot: For a three-point shot, you must be outside the three-point half circle that runs above the lane circle down to the baseline.

Hook Shot: This more advanced shot involves shooting the basketball one-handed from the *opposite* side of your body from the goal, so it sails over your head. It's hard to defend against because the shooter's body is in the way, but it requires a lot of practice.

Bank Shot: When a shot comes off the backboard instead of swishing into the net, it's considered a bank shot; this is the most reliable shot, so it's good to use when you're not sure if you can make it. It works best up close to the goal from underneath. This shot also does a good job of drawing fouls.

Fadeaway: This is similar to a jump shot, but instead of standing straight and firm, lean back and move away from the goal after the ball is released. This shot is tough for a defender to block because you're moving away.

Floater: A floater is a ball with an extreme arc that can go over taller defenders, swishing into the net without ever touching the ring or the backboard. This is an extremely difficult shot to make consistently without a lot of practice.

Dunk: While it can be an effective shot if the player is tall enough, only certain players can perform a dunk, and usually not until late high school or college. It involves dribbling up to within two steps of the goal and jumping up to slam the ball directly into the ring. At that point, players sometimes hang for a second on the ring.

Alley-Oop: This shot requires two players. One throws the ball near the basket, and the second player catches it mid-air and shoots, usually for a dunk. This shot isn't used very often in games, but it looks really impressive when done right!

Free Throw: You should spend a lot of time practicing this shot because it's a chance to get a free point, so you don't want to miss it! Any time a player gets fouled while shooting, they get a chance at a free throw. This shot is taken from the top of the lane, with both teams lined up between the marks on the sides. If the player is fouled while shooting three points, they get three shots; if the player is fouled while shooting two points, they get two shots. Even if a player is fouled but still makes their shot, they get a shot, which is added to the points they already made.

DRILLS FOR PRACTICING DIFFERENT TYPES OF SHOTS

Full-Court Layups: This drill is best when you have multiple people to practice with. Form two lines on each side of the court, usually at half court; one-line dribbles down to do a layup, while the other side comes down to rebound the ball. Afterward, the players switch sides to the back of the line.

Jump Shot Spot Shooting: Pick five spots on the court, taking ten shots from each. The position you play should determine where you focus these shots, but under the goal, at each block, each top corner of the lane, and free throws are all good to practice. For outside players, focus on each low spot near the lane, either inside the three-point line, free throw, or in the middle, inside the three-point line.

Catch and Shoot: Have a partner pass you the ball from the same spots in the drill above and take the shot. Make sure to get these shots off fast, and have your partner come at you like a defender after they pass you the ball.

Free Throws: At each practice, try to shoot at least 40 free throws—practice makes perfect!

Pressure-Free Throws: This drill is designed to recreate the pressure of a real game. Before shooting free throws, assign a penalty. For example, if you're shooting five free throws, each one you miss is a suicide; if your teammates each get two free throws, for every miss, the whole team must run a lap around the court.

Around the World Three Points: Pick five points around the three-point line and shoot from each place until you make a shot. Once you've made them all in one go, go back and shoot at each spot again, but this time, if you miss, move on to the next. Keep shooting until you've made it on the first shot in each spot.

Cone-marked shooting: Choose a few places around the court that bank shots work well from and shoot at each one ten times. If you don't use the backboard, it doesn't count.

Really, just getting out on the court with a ball and practicing your shots is all you need to do. After all, drills won't improve your shot if you don't put in the work!

FOOTWORK IN SHOOTING

One of the fundamentals of basketball is how you place and move your feet. If your weight is in the wrong place, your shot will be off, and you won't have time to correct yourself for a rebound (when the ball misses). Your legs and feet are what fuel each shot to get the ball in, forming a power base. Practicing footwork and quick movements with smooth transitions will improve your shooting abilities.

Agility is something you can improve as you work on shooting. Footwork involves stopping and accelerating quickly, pivoting, and getting higher in the air for clearer shots. A shot is much easier when you have separation from your defender, and you can only create that separation if you're comfortable moving across the court and don't project your next moves.

Here are some basics to keep in mind while on the court:

- When you catch the ball, you dribble, but once you pick the ball up, you can only pivot on one foot. Once you pivot on your foot, you can't change your feet.
- When you're going for a shot, you can take two steps before it's considered traveling. Those steps are usually used for layups, dunks, and hook shots.

SHOOTING UNDER PRESSURE

Staying calm during games is vital. Panicking makes it harder to figure out your next move. It's easy to make all your shots when you're practicing, with no fans, no timer, and no defenders—but making the same shots during a game is much more difficult.

If you feel yourself starting to panic, take a few breaths—not fast ones, deep ones. Deep breaths provide more oxygen and slow your heart rate while breathing rapidly increases your heart rate and can cause hyperventilation.

One way to avoid panic during real-life game situations is to practice; once you take time to calm down, muscle memory should kick in. Repetition is the main goal of practice, and muscle memory develops when you've done something so many times that your body remembers how to do it without even thinking about it.

Free throws put you under pressure, especially if the game is close and time is running out. In situations like that, your team really needs the points. Develop a free throw routine and practice it until you feel confident. Always use the same routine, and that confidence will follow.

When dealing with pressure, visualizing success can play an important role in winning. If you envision yourself making your shots, you're much more likely to succeed than if you doubt yourself. Those positive thoughts and confidence will make you a better player.

Stay calm during games, get some practice in, trust your routines, visualize success, and believe in yourself!

CHAPTER SEVEN: DEFENSIVE SKILLS

While good shooting skills and a strong offense get you the points you need to win the game, you need a solid defense to keep the other team from scoring more than your team.

THE BASICS OF PLAYING DEFENSE

When you're on defense, a defense-ready position allows you to move quickly to guard your player. The faster you can react, the better you'll be able to guard.

Start with your feet shoulder-width apart; bend your ankles, knees, and hips; keep a straight back with your head up and arms wide; and make sure you're balanced.

While defending, watch the *play*, not the ball. Don't trust a player's eyes (as we discussed earlier, they can mislead you), but their torso will often broadcast which direction they intend to move. Your job is to stay between them and the goal, so knowing which direction they're heading is vital.

Don't let your opponent get too far from you; leaving room could give them a chance to shoot. Don't just lean toward or away from your player; make sure you're moving your feet! Follow them as they dance to the side, sliding your feet to keep pace.

Communication with your team is just as important on defense as on offense. If the other team starts setting a "screen," call it out so your teammates don't run into it. A "screen" (or "pick") is when a player stands still and lets their ball handler dribble past them to shake their defender, which can open them up to get clear shots.

Also, let your team know if you need help. Always keep your hands up; when your hands are already up, you'll be quicker to block your opponent. Plus, if you have your hands up and moving, it's harder for your opponent to see what is going on.

STAYING LOW AND BALANCED

A low and balanced stance is important on defense because it allows you to move quickly and keep up with the person you're guarding. You'll be shuffling your feet from side to side in a defensive shuffle, so your knees must be bent, allowing you to jump up when you need to block a ball.

In addition to providing balance, staying low to the ground with a wide, solid base makes it much harder for offensive players to push you around. The low stance gives you more control over your movements, allowing you to pivot and change directions quickly. With a wide and low stance, you're less likely to trip or slip when fast corrections are needed.

TECHNIQUES FOR GUARDING OPPONENTS

Technique is important if you want to keep the other team from scoring. Strong defensive skills make you a valuable player and benefit your entire team. You can be a stronger defensive player in several ways, and your coach will instruct your team on the strategies they want to run.

"Man-to-man" defense is one of the most common types of defense, setting each teammate to guard an offensive player. Sometimes, your coach will assign who they want you to guard, but sometimes, in a fast-paced game, *you'll* be responsible for making your own decisions.

In those situations, you should look for an opponent with the same position. It's easier to guard when you're familiar with the position. Call out the number of the person you've decided to guard so your teammates know, and no one will be left unguarded. Your job is to stop your player from gaining possession, passing the ball, or scoring.

Another common defensive strategy is "zone" defense, where each defender is responsible for a specific area on the court. In this strategy, anyone in your assigned area becomes your responsibility. There are several different varieties of zone defense: the 1-2-2, the 1-3-1, the 3-2, and the 2-3. These numbers refer to the placement of your defenders.

The 3-2 is one of the most common and easy to set up. The "3" refers to the guards that form the top of the defense. These are the point guard, who's responsible for the top of the three-point half circle and the surrounding area, and two shooting guards, responsible for the wing areas on their sides. The "2" refers to two lower players covering post positions under the goal.

In some situations, you'll drop back to past midcourt before you pick up the defense, but in others, your team might try a "full-court press," in which your defense starts on the offense's side of the court in hopes your opponents won't get to the other side before you can gain possession. Remember, it's okay if this is confusing at first—you'll get it soon enough! You can always ask a trusted adult to help you look up videos online, so you can see what these zone defenses look like in play.

BECOMING A GOOD DEFENSIVE PLAYER

Being a good defender involves how you act while you're guarding, no matter what type of defense your team is running. Taking the charge can be hard, but sometimes, it's the only option. When an opponent is charging toward the goal to shoot, get in between them and the goal, then plant your feet and let them hit you. If they knock you down, they'll get a foul; however, if your feet aren't planted, it can be a foul on *you*.

This is hard for two reasons. For one, keeping your feet planted is hard to do when someone is charging at you; for another, it can *hurt* to get knocked down! If you do it correctly, the ball will be given to your team.

Stealing the ball is another way to help your team gain possession. While you're guarding, if you get the opportunity to reach out and snatch the ball, take it! You can't hit the other player, but even if you can't take the ball, it will become a "jump" ball if you both hold on to it.

A jump ball takes place when two opposing players have possession. The ref blows a whistle, and the teams take turns getting the ball.

When you're guarding, and your opponent tries to shoot, it's perfectly fine for you to block their shot. While you can't touch the *player* when they're shooting, you can smack the ball and put it off course. Blocking shots is a great way to keep the other team from scoring.

When you're on defense, you should always be "boxing out." When a shot goes up, turn and put your back to your player and box them out by putting yourself between them and the goal. Bend slightly and use your hips, legs, and outstretched arms to block them so they can't catch the rebound when they miss.

When the ball doesn't go in, someone must catch the rebound. When the ball bounces off the basket or backboard, be ready to jump up and be the first to grab it. Once you have the ball, come down strong with your elbows out. Then, you can pass or dribble to an open spot. Good rebounding gives your team possession more—and the more often your team has the ball, the more chances you have to score.

BLOCKING SHOTS AND STEALING THE BALL

When you're defending, it's important to stay in the correct position so you can react quickly. As usual, stay low with your knees bent so you can watch and predict when your opponent reacts. Sometimes, players will give away their next move with their eyes, but good players know how to trick their defenders, so be careful.

Timing is important; if you jump up too early, the opposing player will get around you, but if you jump too late, the ball will already be gone. It takes practice to develop good timing—and it won't always work—but once you've mastered the skill, it's extremely helpful on the court and looks impressive.

As we mentioned, you should always keep your hands up. It's much faster to have your hands up already than to try to raise them when defending, especially for blocking and stealing.

When you're trying to steal the ball, stay close to the player you're guarding and watch the ball. It's important to be quick when stealing so you can grab and go with the ball. A great time to steal is during a pass because no one controls the ball while it's in the air, so if you can get there, you'll be able to grab the ball.

No matter what you're trying to do as a defensive player, make sure you don't hit the other team's hands or arms, or you'll get a foul!

IMPROVING DEFENSIVE SKILLS

At every practice, you should be doing "defensive slides." Defensive slides allow you to move quickly from side to side so you can keep up with whoever you're guarding. To do this, point your foot in the direction you'll be sliding and use the other leg to push yourself. That way, you can quickly pivot when you need to change directions.

Here are some drills to improve your defensive game:

> **Full Court Zigzag:** Pair off, assigning one player to offense and one to defense. The offensive player dribbles in zigzags down the court while the guard uses defensive slides to stay in front and cut them off. Then, switch and go the other way.
>
> **First to the Ball:** This is a good drill for jumping on defense. You and one other player start at the baseline on either side of the lane, and another person throws, rolls, or bounces the ball. The first person to the ball tries to score, and the other quickly jumps on defense. The drill continues until one of you scores.
>
> **Shifting Team Drill:** You need eight people for this drill, four on defense and four on offense. The offensive players line up at the three-point line, while the defense stays inside

it. The offensive players will swing the ball around so the defense can work together, shifting as the ball moves. Good communication between players is key for this drill.

FOULS AND HOW TO AVOID THEM

Both offensive and defensive players can commit fouls, so you need to know about all of them.

Fouls on a shooting player result in free throws, which can be easy points. If you receive five fouls, you're removed from the game and can't help your team anymore. More serious fouls can result in suspension for more than just that game. Once your team gets so many fouls, it becomes bonus time, and every foul results in a free throw. The number of fouls depends on where you're playing.

Personal Fouls: These are some of the easiest fouls to commit because any time you make illegal contact with an opponent, it's considered a personal foul.

- Holding a player anytime, even if they don't have a ball, is a foul.
- Pushing any player is against the rules and is a foul.
- Blocking someone who is shooting by touching them is a foul.
- Tripping someone from the other team on purpose is a foul.
- Preventing another player from moving by using any part of your body is a foul.

One of the most common of these is "reaching in." It's considered a foul when you're trying to steal the ball and hit your opponent's arm. When attempting to steal the ball, make sure you reach directly for the ball *only* when you see an opening, and don't reach across the other player.

Fouls can result in free throws or a turnover for the other team.

>**Technical Foul:** This foul doesn't involve physical contact. Any time a player displays unsportsmanlike behavior — like foul language, disrespect, arguing with the referee, or a display of anger — it can result in a technical foul. The court is not the place to show when you're upset, so remember to watch your temper!

>**Flagrant Foul:** When it's obvious that a player meant to foul, using violent or unnecessary contact, it's considered a "flagrant" foul. These types of fouls could result in injury, so they're taken very seriously.

Players who commit a flagrant foul are usually removed from the game. Depending on the league, they could even end up removed from the team or suspended for future games. Because of this, it's important to be respectful and stay in control of your emotions.

CHAPTER EIGHT: REBOUNDING SKILLS

Rebounding is a huge part of defense; the better you understand how to catch one, the more effective you'll be on the court.

REBOUNDING IN BASKETBALL

In essence, rebounding is grabbing the ball when someone misses a shot. It doesn't matter which team was shooting; what's important is that your team gets it next! Rebounding can change the game completely, turning a missed shot into a fast break or a chance for your team to score.

When your team is good at rebounding, you can clean up any missed shots and control the game's pace. When you're on offense, your team will get another chance to shoot; When you're on defense, rebounding takes away the other team's chance to shoot again.

POSITIONING AND TIMING FOR REBOUNDS

It's important to be in the right spot and have good timing. Always try to stay between your opponent and the basket so that when the ball bounces off the goal, you can grab it first. When you're waiting to see if a shot goes in, stand with your knees slightly bent in preparation to jump.

Watch the ball's arc to determine where it'll bounce and wait until the ball is coming down to jump up. The farther away a shot is, the farther it will probably bounce back out. Utilize the bouncing-out skills you've been working on to keep the other players away from the ball if necessary.

TECHNIQUES FOR OFFENSIVE AND DEFENSIVE REBOUNDING

Once you've rebounded the ball, what comes next? If you're on offense, you need to go back up for the shot; if your defender is too close, try to get the ball clear. Dribble if you need to make some room for yourself.

However, when you're under the goal, sometimes the area is so congested that dribbling isn't a good option. In this situation, you should look for an open teammate and pass it to them.

When you're on defense and dribbling, the first thing you want to do after rebounding is to secure the ball, making sure no one can take it from you. Then, look for your ball handler or point guard. If *you're* the ball handler or point guard, dribble away from your opponents.

Once the ball is clear, you need to make a fast break or wait for your team to get set up and call a play. Plays are what tell the team where to move so everyone is in the right spot. Knowing what to do after you rebound will help you react more quickly and make sure that you don't waste the opportunity.

DRILLS FOR IMPROVING REBOUNDING SKILLS

Improving Box-Outs: Stand back-to-back with a partner in a defensive stance in the middle of the lane. When your coach blows the whistle, start pushing against each other like you're boxing out an opponent. The first person pushed out loses.

First to the Ball: Pair off and start on opposite sidelines, with the ball in the middle of the court. When the whistle blows, the first one to the ball tries to score while the other player defends.

Rebound Line-Ups: Split the team into two lines of players. Your coach will shoot the ball and miss, then the two players at the front of the line race to rebound the ball, and the player that gets it wins. Continue until everyone's had a chance.

Backboard Rebound: This is a great drill that you can do on your own. Start on one side of the lane and throw the ball up, bouncing it off the backboard. Jump up to catch it mid-air with both hands and come down on the balls of your feet.

Practice Free Throws: Line the team up in free-throw formation, and practice having everyone box out and get to the ball.

Rebound and Layup: Like the backboard rebound, you can do this drill on your own. Stand directly in front of the basket and bounce it off the backboard. Catch the ball mid-air, and without bringing the ball down, lay it back for the shot.

ANTICIPATING WHERE THE BALL WILL GO

If you know where to head for the rebound, there's a better chance you can grab it. If the shot is coming from the left, then there's a good chance the ball will bounce to the right, and vice versa. Spend time watching how the ball bounces off the basket by bouncing it off the goal and seeing where it goes.

When you practice watching the ball, you'll eventually learn to know where to move instinctively. The quicker you get to the ball, the more time you'll have to decide how to handle it!

STAYING MENTALLY FOCUSED

Rebounding is just like all other basketball skills—it's as much about mental focus as physical ability. Staying focused when you play will help you grow your rebounding as much as practice and ability.

When you're focused, you can think quickly, which helps you make the best decision at the moment, giving you more time to make it happen. It can be hard to stay focused during games because fans usually get louder when something exciting happens, but you must learn to tune out the crowd.

Breathing exercises, discussed in Chapter 11, can come in handy here. If you find yourself getting distracted, keep your eye on the ball and take a few slow, deep breaths—in through your nose, out through your mouth—and you'll feel your focus sharpening in no time!

CHAPTER NINE: BOUNCING BACK FROM MISTAKES

Everyone makes mistakes in life, and basketball is no different. How you handle yourself afterward determines what kind of person you will become.

LEARNING FROM MISTAKES

Learning from your mistakes is part of growing up. If you never made any mistakes, you'd never be able to grow and improve. In a game, if you make a mistake—like missing a shot or letting someone score—take time to think back and figure out what you could've done better. Don't dwell on it, though; just file the thought away for later when you can work to improve that shot or skill.

Even professional athletes make mistakes and take time later to work on them. That's how they improve, just like you. Mistakes aren't always a one-time thing, either. You might have a bad game and miss several shots, but that shouldn't stop you from pressing on. Perseverance means continuing to do something, even when it's difficult.

You need to have perseverance when a game isn't going well, and you feel like you keep making mistakes. Everyone has games like that, and they don't define you as a player. Persevering shows dedication because you keep trying to move past those mistakes.

When you do make a mistake, it's important to remember that you're on a team. One person's mistakes don't make or break a game! If you have free throws with no time on the clock, your team is one point down, and you miss them, it *still* isn't your fault—it took the entire team not to be able to pull ahead sooner.

Mistakes will happen in other aspects of your life as well. You might forget to do your homework because you weren't organized, but that's a skill that you can work on and, next time, be more organized. If you get into a fight with a friend or sibling, think about what started it and whether it's worth damaging the relationship with that person; maybe apologizing is the better path. When you make thoughtful decisions, the next time you're in that situation, you'll be slower to react because you learned from it.

MAINTAINING FOCUS AFTER ERRORS

While you need to reflect on mistakes to learn from them, there's a time and place to do it. During the game isn't that time. Staying focused is important; basketball is a fast-paced game, and you can quickly lose track of what's going on or miss another opportunity.

If you find yourself getting distracted after making a mistake, take a few deep breaths and calm yourself. Refocus on the present moment, not what's already happened.

When you find yourself repeatedly struggling to shake off mistakes, you might need to develop a "mistake routine." When you slip up, make a habit of doing something specific afterward to help you let it go. It doesn't need to be anything remarkable; it can be something minor, like clapping your hands a few times or jogging in place. Over time, this ritual will become a way to help you reset your mind and focus so you can get back in the game.

Understanding your role on the team can help you stay focused, too. If you're constantly struggling to figure out where to be or what's happening, talk with your coach. More than likely, they'll be happy to help you understand your responsibilities on the court.

During games, it's important to know where you need to be. If you're in the wrong place on defense, you'll leave a gap for the offense to get through. However, if you're focused and understand your role, you'll be an asset to your team!

STAYING POSITIVE AND MOTIVATED

When you've made a mistake, it can be hard to stay positive and motivated but making a slip-up doesn't mean your overall performance can't be good. Remind yourself that it's all part of the game, and don't be too hard on yourself.

Think about how much effort you put in. Did you try your best and make an honest mistake, or were you slacking off? Most likely, you were giving it your all, and it was an honest mistake. You should feel good about the fact that you gave it your best shot!

Keeping a journal after games and practices can be encouraging. Write down at least three things you did well—it might just be hustling down the court, or you might've been the leading scorer in a game. You can write down as many things as you want to.

Focusing on the positives helps you maintain an optimistic attitude and mindset. Sometimes, just getting it out can help, so talk to your support system if you're feeling down. Your parents, guardians, and friends will be glad to listen and remind you of some of the positive things you've done.

Basketball should be fun, so if you find yourself stressed or feeling negative about it, taking a break might be a good idea. This doesn't mean you won't ever play again; it just allows you to focus on other things for a while.

SUPPORT TEAMMATES AFTER A MISTAKE

We're all human, so you're not the only one who'll make mistakes—your teammates will also slip up occasionally. Supporting them when this happens is an important part of being a good teammate, and it's how a team becomes successful.

When someone misses a shot, instead of criticizing them, tell them it was a good try. If a teammate seems down, remind them of their past successes and good efforts. Sometimes, they might just need to talk about it to move on. Be a good listener and support your teammates by letting them speak.

A good teammate is supportive during both wins and losses, so be there for your fellow players—just like you would want them to be there for you. Encouraging words can make all the difference after a game, so let your positive attitude inspire the rest of your team. Supporting one another makes a team stronger, and a stronger team is harder to beat!

DEVELOPING A GROWTH MINDSET

Having a growth mindset means you avoid looking at things negatively and, instead, believe you can improve with effort and practice. Instead of thinking to yourself, "I'm not good at this," think, "I'm not good at this *yet*." Then, you can focus on practicing instead of giving up. A growth mindset helps you look at mistakes as opportunities to grow instead of disasters.

Another aspect of a growth mindset is being open to feedback. Having room for improvement doesn't mean you're bad at something; it just means you can improve. Ask your coach how you can improve, and they'll be happy to help.

Embrace challenges instead of avoiding them; just because something is hard doesn't mean you can't do it! Having that attitude will help you not only in basketball but also in life. For instance, your grades will go up if you think, "It might be hard, but I can learn this," instead of "I'm dumb," or "This is stupid." Telling yourself that you can succeed with enough hard work and practice is part of a growth mindset.

To help you develop a growth mindset, set goals. When you set your goals, make sure they're realistic. If you set impossible goals, you'll only get discouraged when you can't achieve them.

Go ahead and set some specific goals for yourself. You might consider dribbling back and forth three times with your non-dominant hand without making a mistake, making ten free throws without missing, making a three-pointer, or just running an extra suicide after practice.

BUILDING RESILIENCE AND CONFIDENCE

The more resilience and confidence you have, the easier it is to bounce back from mistakes and focus on building a growth mindset. Resilience is the ability to recover from setbacks or mistakes. It comes when you focus and stay positive, remembering that the setbacks you've encountered are temporary. Focus on your strengths, and don't worry about anything else.

When you run into a challenge, step back and think about possible solutions and how you want to handle it. Giving up easily isn't the answer; use your resilience and confidence to persevere until you overcome the challenges you're faced with.

Be kind to yourself. When your friend or teammate makes a mistake, are you patient and understanding? You owe yourself the same! Mistakes happen, and being kind and understanding to yourself is the best way to handle them. Give yourself the same encouragement and support you would give anyone else.

Having supportive people around you to provide a solid support system makes it easier to build confidence and resilience. Sometimes, you might find that you have a friend or teammate who is constantly tearing you down or making you feel bad. Those people might be jealous, not know how to express their emotions, or just think it's funny. No matter their reasons, it's a good idea to distance yourself so they don't affect your confidence.

No one can be good at everything, so find your strengths and focus on them. While it's important to improve your weaker skills, don't let your shortcomings discourage you. You might be an excellent dribbler but not great at catching rebounds or a great rebounder and struggle with three-pointers. Being a successful basketball player takes many skills, so concentrate on what you're good at.

Resilience is the ability to persevere. When you have clear goals and determination, resilience will help you achieve great things.

Don't be nervous about listening to constructive criticism from coaches and teammates. People who know the game and care about you often provide useful feedback. Listening and acting on their advice can help you improve, so keep a positive attitude and be receptive!

CHAPTER TEN:
GAME STRATEGIES AND TACTICS

When you're playing basketball, it's important to know the rules, learn strategies, and develop effective tactics so you can be an asset on the court.

UNDERSTANDING THE RULES OF BASKETBALL

Offensive Rules

The basics of basketball are pretty straightforward: The game is played with two teams of five players each, and the goal is to score points by shooting the ball into the opponent's basket. The team that gets the most points by the end of the game wins.

If you want to move while you have the ball, you're dribbling or not moving. If you move, you must dribble with one hand at a time. You can't start moving again once you pick the ball up—you must plant one foot and pivot on it.

You'll get a foul for double dribbling if you start dribbling after allowing the ball to rest (even if it's only in one hand) or touch the ball with both hands simultaneously. Another dribbling violation is "carrying". It's similar to a double dribble but carrying involves taking a step while the ball rests in one or both hands.

Once you start dribbling, you must keep it up until you get where you want to go. If you get a foul for double dribbling or carrying, the other team will get the ball—and nobody wants that! However, if you pass the ball to a teammate and they pass it back, it's okay to start dribbling again.

Another way to lose the ball is to let it get out of bounds. When the ball passes outside the boundaries of the court—the end line, baseline, or sidelines—whoever touched it last loses the ball. Then, the other team gets to throw the ball in from whichever line it crossed.

When your team has the chance to pass the ball in from out of bounds, you have a limited amount of time to do it. This time can vary depending on the league you're playing in, but it's normally five seconds. If your team doesn't get the ball in during that time, the other team gets it back.

There are a few fouls your team can commit on offense:

> **Once you pass the half-court, you can't take the ball back across the half-court line.** If you dribble, pass, or pick the ball up behind the midcourt line, you'll get a "backcourt" violation, resulting in a turnover.
>
> **A "moving screen" takes place when you set a screen, and then move to block the opponent** as your teammate comes by with the ball. Your feet must be set in order to set a screen, so if you move, expect a foul.
>
> **Another thing to avoid is trying to jump over someone to grab the ball,** which can put their safety at risk—and get you a foul. Jump *up* for a rebound as much as you want, but if an opponent is in your way, going around them to play defense and try to steal the ball is the best way to do it.

Defensive Rules

For your defense to be effective, you must be aggressive—to a point. While you need to guard your player, trying to gain an advantage with illegal physical contact will get you a foul.

> **"Blocking" is a defensive foul that occurs when you try to block an offensive player from moving** with your body. If you do try to stop someone from moving with your body,

it's considered a personal foul. You'll often have blocking called on you when you try to take a charge without having your feet set.

A "hand check" is another type of foul, where you use your hand or hands to keep an offensive player from moving. If you put your hand on the other player to slow them down or change their direction, it's considered a hand check.

Similar to hand checks is "holding," but it's more obvious because it involves grabbing a player (or their uniform) to physically stop them from moving. Be careful because holding fouls can be committed against *all* offensive players, not just the ball handler.

When you use your hands in a way that isn't allowed, you'll get a foul for "illegal hand use." This can mean hitting a player's arms when they're shooting, resulting in a free throw, or even just putting both hands on an opponent. If you very obviously hit a player, though, it can be a much more serious foul.

BASIC OFFENSIVE AND DEFENSIVE STRATEGIES

Having both offensive and defensive strategies is critical to winning games. For these strategies to work, your team must work together and communicate effectively on the court.

Offensive strategies might include passing, screening, cutting, spacing, shooting, and rebounding:

Passing in a practiced way is called a play, which is how a team moves the ball until there's an opening to shoot. When a play is called, everyone on the team needs to do their job and get to the right place. Talk to your coach if you're unsure how a play works.

Plays can also involve dribbling. For instance, once a play is called, your team might have predetermined places to dribble. You need to know where the ball handler is going so you can cut screens and shake defenders as a team.

Another part of a play can be cutting, which is making sharp, sudden changes in direction to get open for the ball. In a practiced play, the person with the ball will know where the cutter is heading and get the ball there.

Spacing is also crucial — if everyone's on the same side of the court, there's no one to pass to on the other side, which makes it easy for the defense to sweep in and steal the ball.

When you're on defense, it's best to have several different strategies ready. Depending on the team you're playing, man-to-man or zone might be the best defense.

It's good to have strategies for rebounding, as well. When your team is shooting, arrange in advance who will go in for the rebound. Defensively, you should always have people rebounding and trying to grab the ball while it's still in the air.

READING THE GAME AND MAKING QUICK DECISIONS

Keep your head up: When you're on the court, whether you have the ball or not, you should never be looking down. Always have your head up and your eyes moving. It's critical to know where your teammates and opponents are.

Anticipate your opponents: Predicting what your opponents will do next allows you to get there a few seconds sooner, giving you a chance to steal the ball or block the player.

Keep up with the game: What you decide to do will be determined by the score, time remaining, personal fouls, team fouls, and which teammates are in. If you make decisions without knowing what's happening, you'll likely make poor ones.

Stay calm: When the game heats up, don't let it get to you. Pressure can cause you to make mistakes. Keep your breathing steady and keep your cool.

Watch and learn: Take advantage of opportunities to watch more experienced players—the more you know, the better you'll be. Watch college games with more experienced players at your school and ask someone to record your games so you can go back and see where you could improve.

Know the team plays: Each team will have plays that cater to their strengths, so knowing your team's plays is vital. Familiarize yourself with each play and know how to play every position so you can plug in anywhere.

React quickly: Stay on your toes and remain balanced so that when you see an opening, you can react quickly. Not staying balanced slows you down, which makes your reaction time suffer.

COMMUNICATION AND TEAMWORK

Communication helps with your team's coordination on the court. You can call out plays, call for screens, and let your teammates know you're open. The more effectively your team communicates, the better you'll work in sync. When your team is on defense, you can warn about screens, call to switch, ask for help, and tell your team which opponent you're guarding.

Encouragement and positive motivation can be just as important on the court. Boost your team's morale by telling teammates, "Good job!" or, if needed, encouraging them by saying, "Keep your head up!"

Good communication helps your team avoid turnovers and holes in your defense. A good defense is just as important as any other skill on the court.

A team that works together well shares the same goals and works together toward winning. Teamwork and being supportive of one another will help you achieve more than you ever could alone.

Finding ways to improve your communication skills as a team is important. The best way to develop this is practice—the more you practice, the more you'll instinctively know how to react on the court. The more you practice together, the better you'll work as a unit.

Don't just practice, though; spend time together as a team in different settings. Find activities to do together, like going out to eat as a team to get to know each other off the court. Hold team meetings to review footage, discuss your weaknesses, and plan strategies.

As discussed in Chapter 5, communication doesn't just have to be verbal; Teams work out hand signals for plays and common setups. This not only makes it hard for your opponents to anticipate what you're doing, but it also works well in intense game situations. In a close game, the crowd can get loud when tensions are high, making it hard to hear your teammates—and this is the perfect time to use those nonverbal cues!

DIFFERENT PLAYER POSITIONS AND ROLES

There are many positions on a basketball court, each of which is important. Each role contributes different skills, and understanding the responsibilities of each role makes you a more versatile player.

> **Point guards** are often considered the leaders on offense because they call the plays. As a point guard, you'll be responsible for bringing the ball down the court, calling out offensive plays, and making sure that the ball gets into play.
>
> As a point guard, you'll need amazing dribbling skills, good decision-making skills, strong passing skills, and the ability to see the entire court at once and pay attention to where everyone is.
>
> **A shooting guard** is another player who plays out wide and is a big scorer. One of their primary responsibilities is helping move the ball to keep it from getting trapped in a corner or prevent the team from losing the ball before someone gets open for a shot.

As a shooting guard, you need to be able to shoot from the three-point line, have good ball-handling skills, be able to drive to the goal, and have strong outside defense.

A small forward, or "three," is a player who needs to be able to shoot from inside or outside. It's one of the more versatile positions on the team that needs to be able to fill in anywhere on the court.

As a small forward, you'll need the ability to shoot from anywhere on the court, strong defensive skills, a sense of rebounding, and quick decision-making.

The power forward is one of the strongest players on the team, usually one of the taller ones. Their job is to stay close to the basket, scoring from rebounds and passes.

Power forwards need to be bigger players, so they don't get pushed around under the goal. Good rebounding is one of the skills you'll need, along with under-goal shots. Being a strong defensive player is also important, and the ability to set good screens is helpful.

The center is usually the tallest player on the team, so they can play under the goal. They must block shots and be the top rebounders and highest under-goal scorers.

As a center, you'll need height and strength, the ability to block shots, excellent rebounding skills, and the ability to control the defense under the goal.

While you'll probably play many different positions, starting with one and mastering it can help you earn a spot on the starting team.

DEVELOPING A GAME PLAN WITH YOUR COACH

Talking to your coach about your short- and long-term goals can help you stay on track. In the short term, you need to figure out skill development, conditioning, and knowledge.

Your skill development should focus on your strengths so you can be exceptional with them, but you should also work on improving your weaker skills. Having a plan helps you improve all your skills, not just the ones that come naturally.

Conditioning is a vital part of being a basketball player. You need the stamina to keep going for the entire game without getting winded. You need to be strong enough to power your way through without being pushed around the court. Agility lets you move quickly and react quickly.

Ask your coach to help you set goals and provide drills to increase your skills. Having your coach help you stay on track makes it easier to stay accountable. Consistency is key; your coach can tell you how often to practice each exercise. There is such a thing as too much, so having someone who can help you moderate avoids burnout.

Tracking your progress is an important part of any game plan, too. Whether you decide to use a physical journal or something electronic, you should record your progress regularly. Track things like free throw, three-point, and other shooting percentages, the time of your dribbling drills, running times, and weightlifting numbers.

Not only can your coach help you set goals for improvement, but they can also help you find the best path forward. If you want to make the varsity team or even play college ball, talk to your coach so they can help you.

CHAPTER ELEVEN: MENTAL TOUGHNESS

We've talked about mental toughness and how important it is, but how do you overcome pressure to achieve it? In this chapter, we'll talk about how to handle these extreme emotions.

MENTAL TOUGHNESS IN BASKETBALL

Mental toughness helps you stay focused, which is important in a fast-paced sport where everything changes quickly. Focus allows you to block out distractions from the crowd or boos from the other team. When pressure and stress start to slow you down and affect the way you play, mental toughness will help you get back on track.

Confidence also comes from mental toughness because you believe in your abilities without doubting that you'll play well. That confidence allows you to act quickly, take that important shot, or lead an impressive play.

Resilience is also part of mental toughness. Setbacks are part of the game, no matter how good a player you are. You'll miss shots and let opponents score on you, but that doesn't determine what kind of player you are—the ability to shake it off and move forward does.

Developing these traits takes time but keeping them in mind will help you become a better player in the long run.

HANDLING PRESSURE AND STRESS

When you're starting to feel stressed, it's time to focus on the moment, not the end goal. Sometimes, you might get so worried about winning that you lose track of what's happening. When you feel anxious, don't think about the end results; think about what you need to do *right now*.

Instead of needing 20 points to tie, think, "I need to make a shot on this play and try to steal it back on defense." Focusing on the immediate plan helps manage your stress so you don't get overwhelmed.

Just like any skill, the more you practice, the better you get at handling pressure. Try to create high-stress situations in practice. Use scrimmages, timers, and penalties to make it feel more intense. Shoot ten free throws and make yourself run a lap for each one you miss. Time yourself doing dribbling maneuvers and keep trying to beat your previous time.

The way you encourage your teammates is also how you need to encourage yourself. Use those positive thoughts to push through high-pressure moments. When you're on the line to shoot a free throw at the end of the game, and your team is down one, remember how good you are at free throws and how many you've made; this is just another one.

Deep breathing—in through your nose and out through your mouth—can make a big difference. When panic sets in, you start to breathe fast, which can lead to hyperventilating and getting lightheaded.

Slow breathing calms the nervous system and reduces stress hormones in the body. Try some deep breathing exercises, and you'll find they help you calm down.

Just like you don't need to worry about the end of the game, you also need to avoid dwelling on past mistakes. If you're more worried about your mistakes than how you will play in the next few minutes, you're letting stress take over. Stay in the moment.

Trust the hard work you've put in. Training and practicing prepare you for high-pressure moments, so you'll have instinct and experience to fall back on. Skills and strategies that your team has worked out make all the difference in a high-pressure game.

OVERCOMING MISTAKES AND SETBACKS

While mistakes and setbacks are part of the game, they can still be discouraging. It's easy to say, "Don't let mistakes drag you down," but what are some real ways to accomplish that?

We've said it before, but it's important: Learn from them! Every time you make a mistake, it's an opportunity to learn. Avoid getting upset, using stress-management techniques to focus on the future and the positive.

Have a short memory for mistakes. There's no need to file them away in your long-term memory; think about them, realize what you can learn from them, and then let them go. You wouldn't hold a teammate accountable for every little mistake they make, so give yourself the same grace.

Keep practicing focusing on your weak areas, and those setbacks will become a thing of the past!

VISUALIZATION AND MENTAL REHEARSAL

Before each game or big event, imagine the outcome you want. Take a few minutes before the game and think about what this game looks like to you. Run through the plays and moves you want to use during the game in your mind: the shots you're going to make, the defensive skills you'll put to the test, and the results you want.

Mentally practicing before a game motivates you to go and put what you envision on the court, helping to reinforce your physical skills and improve your mental toughness. The feeling of success and confidence that comes from winning a game is the feeling you need to walk onto the court with because *that* is a winning attitude.

DEALING WITH PERFORMANCE ANXIETY

Anxiety is common in high-emotion situations. It's okay if you feel that way, but there are ways to deal with it.

So, what does anxiety *feel* like, mentally and physically? Anxiety causes feelings of panic or fear. If you feel irritable or snappy before a game, it might be because of anxiety. It can cause your jaw to clench, shoulders to bunch up, headaches, nervous fidgeting, sweaty hands, or nausea.

Knowing what anxiety looks like can help you avoid it, but it can also help you identify it in your teammates. There might be someone dealing with anxiety who just needs some positive encouragement.

Turn that overwhelming anxiety into an edge that can help you stay sharp and focused by using relaxation techniques.

USING RELAXATION TECHNIQUES

Deep breathing is a valuable tool, as you read before. Find somewhere comfortable to sit, inhale deeply through your nose and into your stomach or diaphragm, hold that breath for a moment, and release it slowly through your mouth.

This is a great technique to use before games, during game breaks, before big tests, during social interactions, and any other time in your life when you feel anxiety creeping up on you.

Muscle relaxation is another way to relax your body and mind. Tense muscles tell your brain something is wrong, so focus on different muscle groups and consciously relax them. Start with your toes, curling them up tightly for 10 seconds, then relax them. Move up to the muscles in both legs, then do your stomach, chest, and arms before moving to your neck and face.

If you ever catch yourself feeling tense, use this technique, and your mind will relax along with your body.

Using visualization to relax involves closing your eyes and imagining a peaceful scene. It could be the beach, lake, forest, mountains, or your bedroom—just imagine that place. Focus on what it looks like, then imagine the sounds and smells you associate with that place.

You should do this in a quiet place, so outside noises won't distract you. Being comfortable also helps you focus on what's going on in your mind and not around you. Spend several minutes in your new mindscape, and let the familiarity relax you.

WHEN TO GET HELP

Playing basketball and other sports has many incredible benefits, helping you stay healthy and in shape while bringing you closer to your teammates. However, with all the benefits of sports, they can come with a lot of stress, adding to an already stressful social and academic life.

It's normal to experience some stress, especially around game time or when big events, like tournaments, are coming up. The important thing is to know when to get help because the stress is becoming too much.

Stress can cause headaches, stomach problems, and trouble sleeping at night, along with intense negative emotions like anger or sadness. If you feel like stress is getting the best of you, there are several things you can do.

The first step is to talk to a trusted adult you're comfortable with. Whether it's a coach, teacher, parent, or counselor, they can help you decide what steps to take.

If you constantly worry, feel overwhelmed, or lose interest in things you usually enjoy, it might be time to take a break. An adult can help you decide if you've reached that point or how to avoid getting that stressed.

With support, you can continue with all the activities you love with less stress so you can continue to enjoy them!

CHAPTER TWELVE: HEALTHY HABITS

You can't play your best game unless your body is in tip-top shape, so treating your body right is important. A balanced diet helps you be the best player you can be. Still, healthy habits aren't just about what you eat—they also involve getting enough rest and balancing basketball with all your other responsibilities

NUTRITION YOUR BODY NEEDS

There are five main food groups; unfortunately, candy isn't one of them! Each of the five groups provides different benefits for your body, and a balanced diet is the key to good nutrition.

Fruits and Vegetables

Fruits and vegetables provide essential nutrition, like fiber, vitamins, and minerals. Fruits and vegetables contain vitamin C, vitamin A, folate, and potassium. Fiber is necessary because it keeps you from feeling hungry too soon and maintains a healthy stomach and digestive tract.

You need at least five servings of fruits and veggies a day. One serving is considered an apple, an orange, four strawberries, a cup of lettuce, a carrot—about a cup.

Raw food is always good for you, but cooked vegetables also contain healthy fuel for your body. Peas, zucchini, potatoes, peppers, and spinach are all good options.

Grains

The following food group is grains, and most importantly, *whole* grains. Grains contain fiber and antioxidants, along with vitamins and minerals. When picking out grains or bread, look for whole wheat, brown rice, quinoa, and barley.

Barley is one of the healthiest grains you can eat. Look for it in soups, chicken dishes, or even barley tea. Quinoa is easy and quick to prepare, with good protein and magnesium. Try eating it instead of rice!

Replacing white bread with whole wheat or white rice with brown rice or quinoa is a simple way to improve your meals. These aren't your only options for whole grains, either; there's also teff, buckwheat, amaranth, and farro.

Where you live and what your family traditionally eats can affect which grains are available to you, so talk to your parents or guardians to plan some healthy meals.

Protein

Protein is one of the most essential food groups for athletes. Protein builds and maintains your muscles, bones, and tendons. When you're trying to build muscle, you won't be able to do it without protein.

Protein foods are lean meats, fish and other seafood, eggs, nuts, and seeds. It's important to eat at least 50 grams of protein a day. Anywhere from 10-35 percent of your daily calories should come from protein.

Some foods with a lot of protein are chicken breasts, salmon, beef, and tofu. Eating protein won't give you big muscles, but it provides the building blocks you need to grow muscles as you work out.

Dairy

Dairy or dairy-like foods are important, especially as a teenager, and drinking milk is another good source of protein and vitamins.

Not everyone can process dairy, though, as some people are lactose intolerant. You should talk to your doctor if eating or drinking dairy products makes you nauseous or causes stomach pains. Lactose-free milk or dairy alternatives can provide the nutrients you need.

Yogurt and cheese are good sources of dairy. Look for Greek yogurt and avoid products that have candy or sweets added to them. While they might be delicious, the added sugar isn't healthy.

Fats and oils are also important in moderation because they help our bodies absorb vitamins like A, D, and E and aid cell growth and brain health. Look for healthy fats like monounsaturated or polyunsaturated fats, along with omega-3 fatty acids.

DON'T SKIP BREAKFAST!

About a third of preteens and teenagers skip breakfast, but it's important that you don't.

It might be that you don't like breakfast foods, don't have time, or are trying not to gain weight, but no matter what, you need to rethink your morning routine if you aren't eating breakfast. Not eating breakfast can lead to obesity and energy crashes throughout the day.

If you don't like breakfast foods, think outside the box. Not everyone eats eggs, yogurt, or sausage for breakfast! In India, potato curry is a common breakfast; in Morocco, barley soup is a breakfast staple; Brazilians eat fruit or cheesy rolls; and Malaysians sometimes eat sweet coconut rice topped with peanuts, eggs, or cucumber and wrapped in a banana leaf to take it on the go.

Try thinking outside the box, finding food you like without worrying about what's considered "breakfast" food. If you don't have time for breakfast and getting up earlier isn't an option, look for foods you can take with you; protein bars are a great option.

You can also meal-prep breakfast for yourself. The night before, make breakfast sandwiches, cook eggs and sausage so you can just pop them in the microwave, or make overnight oats.

To make overnight oats, use a half cup of rolled oats and a cup of whatever kind of milk you like. Put the ingredients into a container and let them sit in the fridge for at least two hours. The great thing about overnight oats is that you can add any ingredients you want! Try adding peanut butter and some fruit for a PB&J flavor or diced apples, pecans, brown sugar, and cinnamon to make oatmeal apple pie. Experiment and see what oatmeal you like the best!

FOODS TO EAT BEFORE A GAME

Before a big game, you need to eat foods high in carbohydrates, protein, and healthy fats. When you don't give your body the proper fuel, you might notice fatigue, muscle weakness, or nausea. You work hard to be your best at basketball, so it isn't fair to you not to give your body the fuel it needs to perform well.

The night before, eat a high-carb meal like chicken, brown rice, or whole-wheat pasta. These carbs will give you steady energy for the next day. Then, eat a meal about four hours before the game. This gives you time to digest so your body can turn it into fuel. Chicken, fish, and sandwiches are great options. Don't forget to eat some vegetables with your meal!

As you get closer to game time, start cutting out protein, fiber, and fat—they take longer for your body to digest. Make sure you drink plenty of water to hydrate leading up to the game, starting the day before. You should always drink water, but you should drink extra leading up to high-energy events.

Have a healthy meal a couple of hours after the game as well to help your body recover and avoid sluggish feelings the next day.

AWESOME SNACKS TO PACK

About an hour before the game, have a low-fat, low-protein snack so you don't feel sick once you start getting warmed up. Fresh fruits like watermelon, oranges, pineapple, or apples provide natural sugars that convert into energy quickly. The fruit can be fresh or dried if it doesn't have added sugar. Bananas are a great snack, too, because they provide electrolytes and potassium that will prevent cramps while you're playing.

Peanut butter is another good snack that provides long-lasting energy. It also helps maintain your blood sugar levels, so it's a good after-game snack. Try eating a piece of whole wheat toast with peanut butter or almond butter on it.

Pretzels have just enough salt to replace the sodium you lose while sweating. Trail mix can have pretzels and nuts, making it a good snack. Dry whole-grain cereal is also an excellent snack to have with you. You can also put cheese or hummus on a whole-grain cracker for a good snack, though these need to be kept cold.

It's a good idea to plan out pregame meals and prepare snacks so you can have a trial run. Try out foods before practice and see how you feel. If you don't feel awesome, start trading out foods to find the perfect combination.

MANAGING YOUR TIME AND BALANCING LIFE

While playing basketball is a big part of your life, it's important to remember that it's not the *only* part. If you neglect the rest of your life, you'll suffer for it in the long run.

Figure out your priorities. Family, friends, schoolwork, hobbies, relaxation time, other extracurriculars, and basketball should all be considered. Consider how much time you have and decide where you need to spend it.

Your family needs to be a priority because, while you might only play basketball until you graduate from high school, maybe through college or even professionally, it's not a permanent part of your life. Your family will always be there; you need their support to succeed.

Set aside time for your family by eating dinner with them or finding a game everyone enjoys playing. If Sunday is family day, don't schedule anything else. Wherever you can carve out some time to spend with your family, do it! Family time is important for your happiness and feeling loved.

Relaxation is also essential for a well-balanced life. Take time each night to decide how to unwind for the day. Some people like to read for a while, others enjoy a hot bath, some have an evening self-care routine, and others want to listen to relaxing music while solving a puzzle. Do whatever works for you and make it a priority to set time aside for it regularly.

While you've devoted some time and energy to basketball, you must also put that same energy into your schoolwork. Making sure you have designated homework and study time is critical. If your grades drop low enough, you won't be able to play school basketball, and you won't be able to get into a college to play ball. School and grades need to be priorities.

Other hobbies and extracurriculars are also something you should consider. You never know when you might find another passion unless you try out different things. Don't miss out on all the wonderful experiences just because you play basketball.

Talk to a parent, teacher, coach, or other trusted adult if you feel overwhelmed. They can help you figure out how to balance everything you want to do.

CHAPTER THIRTEEN: PLAYING WITH RESPECT AND GOOD SPORTSMANSHIP

There's no point in playing a sport unless you're going to be a good sport. It doesn't matter what your skill level is; playing well means you show good sportsmanship, encourage other players, and treat them with respect.

Sportsmanship is how you play the game and treat your fellow players. It's not always about having the most points or being the best defensive player; it's about how you act while doing it.

RESPECTING OPPONENTS, COACHES, AND REFEREES

Knowing how to show respect is essential and critical to sportsmanship. Your opponents aren't villains or enemies—they're people who love the game of basketball just as much as you do! They worked hard and want to win as badly as you do. Make sure to shake hands after a game and before, if the opportunity comes up, and congratulate them on a good game afterward.

Do not engage in trash talk! It doesn't help you win, and it makes you look bad. During games, the crowd will boo or yell but don't join them. Be respectful—you're representing yourself, your parents, your coach, your school, and your teammates.

If a player gets knocked down or falls, offer a helping hand to get them back up. Avoid taking unfair advantage and try to keep the game fair.

Your coach wants to help you improve and succeed at basketball; that's how they grow. Listen to your coach, do as they say, and thank them for all the energy and effort they put into guiding you and your team.

Asking your coach for feedback can also show respect because it shows them you value their opinion. Be open-minded about their comments, and don't let any previous opinions keep you from following your coach's instructions.

Referees are human and might make mistakes while calling a game; however, they aren't there to *make* you lose, so you should always be respectful—even if you disagree with a call. The next time there's a close call, they're more likely to call for you if you've been respectful and understanding.

HANDLING WINS AND LOSSES GRACEFULLY

Winning a game, especially a hard one, is a fantastic feeling. How you handle yourself after a big win or a hard loss is important. Celebrating a victory with your teammates is fine but save it for the locker room. Don't carry on when you're still on the court or talk down to the losing team. As excited as you are, they're probably just as disappointed. Encourage your opponents, making sure they know they played a good game, even though they didn't win.

While winning is a great feeling, losing can be the worst. In sports, though, there's always a winner and a loser, and you won't always be on the same side. Don't show anger on the court—if you're upset, take it to the locker room. The court isn't the place to show your feelings and disappointment.

Tell the other team, "Good job," and use that positive attitude to bounce back. There will always be other games, but you can't change how you acted in the past.

BUILDING TEAM SPIRIT

While it's important to respect your opponents, coach, referees, and audience, it's just as important to show good sportsmanship to your teammates! No one person can win at basketball—it takes a team. If you aren't being a good teammate, your teammates won't want to play with you. That means they won't pass you the ball and might even ignore you completely.

One way to show respect to your teammates is through encouragement. Whether you're in the game or on the bench, make sure you support your teammates. Simple encouragement can boost your team's confidence, making each player stronger.

Show your support by not getting mad when mistakes are made. After all, you'll make mistakes or bad calls, too, and will appreciate grace and understanding from your teammates. No one is perfect, so set the by encouraging and supporting everyone.

Team spirit is determined by how well your team works together and how much fun you have playing together. Spending time together off the court is an excellent way to build a sense of team spirit. Maybe you sit with different team members occasionally at lunch, or the whole team sits together.

Weekend events are also a great chance to get to know your teammates outside of school and strengthen the bonds between you. One of the benefits of playing basketball and other sports is the chance to make new friends, so take advantage of it!

DEALING WITH CONFLICTS

Conflict is inevitable in basketball because it's a competitive sport. Tempers can run hot, so make sure you're prepared.

If a conflict comes up, stay calm. No matter how angry you are, it's never okay to speak in anger, so take a deep breath before you speak so you don't regret what you say later.

Talking is usually the fastest way to resolve any issue. When you keep an open mind, solutions are easier to find. Make sure you consider both sides because you won't be able to resolve anything otherwise.

However, talking sometimes only escalates the problem, so ask for help if needed. Getting a coach or other adult involved to play mediator can be a good idea. A mediator helps people get along and come to a happy resolution.

Finally, once the conflict has been resolved, *move on*. Don't hold grudges or bring the problem back up later. No one wants to be known as resentful or petty, after all!

BEING A POSITIVE ROLE MODEL

Being a good role model is essential, both on and off the court. That means being someone others look up to, respect, and want to be like.

On the court, lead by example by always practicing good sportsmanship. The respect you show your teammates, opponents, coaches, referees, and fans helps establish what kind of role model you'll become.

Always follow the rules and give your best effort during every game and practice. Being a role model on the court, you help set the tone for the rest of the team. Your teammates will want to follow your lead when they see you working and practicing hard.

Lift up your teammates to have positive energy for everyone. When people hear you using encouraging words, they'll also start to use them.

While demonstrating good sportsmanship is good practice on the court, it's just as important to be a good role model in your personal life. Treating everyone with respect is part of that. Listen actively, be polite, and help out—whether around your house or at school—without being asked. Making good choices is a big part of being a positive role model.

Being kind is another powerful way to lead by example. Kindness is contagious, so spread it wherever you go! Help a friend with schoolwork, give genuine compliments, and say something kind. Even the simplest act of kindness can make someone's day better.

LIFELONG BENEFITS OF PLAYING SPORTS WITH INTEGRITY

Playing sports is fun but playing with integrity makes sports unique. Integrity involves being honest, fair, and respectful in *all* areas of your life. Integrity is part of the foundation of strong character. Always telling the truth will gain you a reputation for being trustworthy, a quality people admire. Start now, and you'll gain people's trust throughout your life.

Building strong relationships in all aspects of life becomes easier when people respect and trust you. People with integrity form stronger connections because of their positive influence in every part of their lives, not just sports.

You can inspire people around you, including friends, teammates, and younger kids who are watching to learn from you. How you play today determines who you become tomorrow.

CHAPTER FOURTEEN: LEGENDS OF THE GAME

Every basketball player dreams of becoming a professional whose name is recognized by fans everywhere. While not everyone becomes a big name, some players have the talent and dedication to make it. Knowing who they are and what makes them great can help you decide what kind of future you want with basketball. Players become famous because of their excellent skills, hard work, and the legacy they leave for the game.

BASKETBALL SUPERSTARS

Michael Jordan has been called the greatest basketball player of all time. He played for the Washington Wizards and Chicago Bulls during his professional career. Over the years, Jordan won six NBA championships, four gold medals with USA Basketball—two of which were Olympic golds—and received the title USA Basketball Male Athlete of the Year. Fans could always count on Jordan for his high-scoring, gravity-defying dunks and crunch-time performances.

LeBron James is considered highly controversial, but he's one of the best players in the game right now. He has played for the Cleveland Cavaliers, the Miami Heat, and the Los Angeles Lakers. LeBron is a versatile player, able to go wherever he's needed. Few players can match his ball-handling, powerful dunks, well-timed passing, and overall presence on the court. Undoubtedly, he's won more games, received more recognition, and scored more points than most other players ever will.

Kobe Bryant played for the Los Angeles Lakers, winning five NBA championships. He was also an 18-time All-Star and 15-time member of the All-NBA team. Kobe is known for signature moves that are nearly impossible to defend against.

Stephen Curry is a well-known three-point shooter who changed how games were played. He's played for the Golden State Warriors since 2009, winning four NBA championships. With an almost 25-point average per game, he's a pivotal player anytime he is on the court.

Diana Taurasi has played for the Phoenix Mercury since 2004. She has averaged over 19 points per game, taking her team to three championships while winning MVP. With 9,000 points, she's an all-time leading scorer for the WNBA and has made the All-WNBA First Team ten times.

EPIC COMPETITIONS AND HISTORIC GAMES

In the 1998 NBA Finals, Michael Jordan led the Chicago Bulls to an unexpected win against the Utah Jazz, securing the Bulls' sixth championship. The Bulls only needed one more win to take the title, so both teams played their hardest until the game was down to 41 seconds. The Bulls were behind by three points when Jordan took control of the game and scored, leaving them only one point behind. At just 5.2 seconds, Jordan stole the ball from Karl Malone and made it down the court for a perfect jump shot.

Game 7 of the 2016 NBA Finals between the Cleveland Cavaliers and the Golden State Warriors was another jaw-dropping game. The Warriors had set a record for the most wins in a season, while the Cavaliers hoped to secure their first championship. The winner of the game would take home the title, and the game was tied until LeBron James blocked a shot with a signature move, getting the ball to Kyrie Irving, who made a three-point shot and took the lead with less than a minute left in the game. With good defense, the Cavaliers took home the title.

Another game of note was Game 6 of the 1980 NBA Finals, between the Los Angeles Lakers and the Philadelphia 76ers. The Lakers only needed one more win to take the championship, but their star player, Kareem Abdul-Jabbar, had been injured and wouldn't be in the game. Magic Johnson was a rookie who usually played as a guard, but he stepped in to play center, leading the game. He made 42 points, 15 rebounds, and seven assists in the process. The game is remembered for this remarkable turn of events, in which an unexpected player stepped up to take the lead.

RECORD-BREAKING MOMENTS

Most Points Per Game

Wilt Chamberlain set a record on March 2, 1962, by scoring 100 points while playing for the Philadelphia Warriors against the New York Knicks. Chamberlain is known for having one of the most impressive records in sports history, and no one has come close to beating his record, with Kobe Bryant coming in second with 81 points.

Most Scoring Titles

Scoring titles are awarded for having the highest average for points per game over a season, and Michael Jordan holds the record for most. He led in scoring for the NBA for ten seasons, which is one of the reasons he's considered one of the best players in sports history.

Three-Point Record

Stephen Curry is well-known for his three-point shooting, and for good reason: Curry holds the record for three-pointers. In 2015-2016, he set a new season record by scoring 402 three-point shots in one season.

All-Time Playoff Points

LeBron James is a well-known player who always shows his skills in the playoffs. He holds the record for the most points scored in championships with 8,162 points.

FAMOUS COACHES

While not as well-known, basketball coaches have stories as incredible as players. It takes a truly talented person to pass the skills of basketball along.

Phil Jackson coached the Chicago Bulls and Los Angeles Lakers and is considered one of the best coaches in the history of the NBA. He won 11 championships and is best known for his triangle offense. He coached players like Michael Jordan, Kobe Bryant, and Shaquille O'Neal.

Pat Summit coached the University of Tennessee's women's basketball team and won eight NCAA championships, making her one of the greatest coaches in college basketball history. She inspired many players and was well-known for being able to develop skills.

Gregg Popovich, nicknamed "Coach Pop," is a longtime coach for the San Antonio Spurs. He has won five championships and the most wins of any coach in NBA history. His coaching includes amazing strategies and pushing players to get the best out of them. He is the reason the Spurs are regarded as such an amazing team.

Mike Krzyzewski coached the Duke University men's team, leading the charge to five NCAA championships. He has an amazing talent for developing players and making them stars. He has even coached the US men's national team to three Olympic gold medals.

Red Auerbach coached the Boston Celtics in the 1950s and 1960s. He led the team to nine NBA championships, making him a pioneer for basketball and a huge influence on how the game is played today. Red was known for his cutting-edge coaching techniques and for putting together strong, winning teams.

LEGENDARY PLACES TO PLAY

When playing basketball, there are many legendary places to play. Here are some that will make your bucket list to attend a game as a professional player, streetball player, or fan.

Madison Square Garden in New York City is one of the most famous basketball courts in the world. It's home to the New York Knicks and has an amazing history; some of the greatest players have played there.

Formerly The Staples Center in Los Angeles, the Crypto.com Arena is home to the Lakers and the Clippers. It's an up-to-date arena with amazing energy, providing a thrill for players and fans alike. Famous players, including LeBron James, have played amazing games there.

In Harlem, New York, Rucker Park started holding tournaments in 1950, and this is where some of the biggest names in basketball started. The court helped jumpstart big names like Wilt Chamberlain, Kareem Abdul-Jabbar, and Julius Erving.

The courts at Venice Beach in Los Angeles sit beachside and attract players from all over to join the games. It's a fun and competitive place to get basketball practice right by the ocean.

The United Center in Chicago is home to the Chicago Bulls and is known for being where Michael Jordan led the Bulls to several championships. It's a great place to join the crowd and feel the excitement of the game.

For players of all ages and skill levels, Basketball City in New York City is a popular place for tournaments, pickup games, and local leagues. It's a 7,000-square-foot, top-of-the-line facility with seven temperature-controlled courts.

IMPACT OF PLAYERS BEYOND THE COURT

Basketball players not only entertain fans and strive to set new records; they can also have an amazing impact off the court, helping their communities, supporting and starting charities, and inspiring people everywhere.

Many famous basketball players trade in their fame and fortunes to support charities of their choice. Some have causes that are important to them, like LeBron James, who established the LeBron James Family Foundation. The foundation focuses on helping kids in LeBron's hometown of Akron, Ohio, by offering scholarships and building schools where they're needed.

Stephen Curry is part of United to Beat Malaria (formerly Nothing But Nets), a foundation that helps provide mosquito nets to low-income families in Africa. Mosquitoes carry malaria, which can be deadly, and the nets protect people from malaria-carrying mosquitoes.

Basketball players are known for helping causes both locally and internationally in ways they wouldn't be able to if not for the fame and money they gained from playing basketball. They put in hard work so that they could help others.

CONCLUSION

Congratulations on finishing this book and taking your first steps toward becoming a great basketball player! From the history of basketball to the skills you'll need to stay healthy and how to be a leader on and off the court, you now have the knowledge you need to succeed.

You've learned that basketball isn't just about winning games; it's also about growing as a person, so focus on the discipline and perseverance you've read about. Encouragement, positivity, and leadership qualities are important, not just on the court, but in all areas of your life. Use these skills in school, with friends, at home, and wherever life might lead you.

Practice your skills regularly—it takes hard work to master anything, and now that you know how to improve these skills, there's no excuse not to get up and work on them! In the process, remember to balance sports and the other aspects of your life, maintain your health, and stay hydrated. Basketball isn't the only important thing in your life, so work hard but don't neglect other important things.

Remember all the famous athletes and coaches who persevered to get where they did; if that's where you want to go, you'll have to work just as hard as they did. Focus on the courts you want to play on in the future and where you want to go as a basketball player, so you'll know what you're working toward.

However, if you're playing because you enjoy basketball and don't plan to continue after high school, that's all right! The skills you've learned in this book will help you play your best, regardless of where you think you'll end up. Now, go out there and play ball!

www.ingramcontent.com/pod-product-compliance
Lightning Source LLC
Chambersburg PA
CBHW070107080526
44586CB00013B/1220